THE

MILLIONAIRE

MOSES

THE MILLIONAIRE MOSES

HIS PROSPERITY SECRETS FOR YOU!

CATHERINE PONDER

"THE MILLIONAIRES OF THE BIBLE"
Series

Published by
DeVORSS & COMPANY
P.O. Box 550, Marina del Rey, Ca. 90294

Library of Congress Catalog Card No. 77-071459

ISBN: 0-87516-232-0

Printed in the United States of America

CONTENTS

INTRODUCTION: YOUR PROSPERITY IS UNLIMITED! 1
    A Special Message From The Author

    "Prosperity Unlimited" began during a recession. How the author prospered. How this book can prosper you. Meet the millionaire Moses. A prosperity invitation to you.

1. PROSPERITY IN THREE PARTS FOR YOU 9

    The millionaire Moses. Prosperity in the first period. How Moses' Egyptian experience can prosper you. Prosperity in the second period. What Moses' Midian Desert experiences mean to you. How intuition prospered a businessman. How Moses' intuition prospered two million people. Moses' mission was to reveal your divine nature. How to use your rod of power successfully. How to bring vast improvement into your life. How they became millionaires. Prosperity in the third period. How Moses' wilderness experience can prosper you. The prosperity mission of Moses. Your prosperity mission. Why some never get into the Promised Land.

2. THE PROSPERITY LAW OF CAUSE AND EFFECT 33

    Why she had eye trouble. How another's eyes were healed. Meet the prosperous mystic. Nothing new about this prosperity symbology. No one can withhold your good. How good things happened to the Author. Gain control of your world through words. How he went from $6,500 to a $30,000 income. One of Moses' greatest prosperity secrets. How a marriage was restored after eleven years' separation. The path to permanently increasing prosperity A meditation to help you use the prosperity law of cause and effect.

3. THE PROSPERITY LAW OF FEARLESSNESS 48

How to get out of bondage. How marriage came to a widow. The prosperity power of persistence. How the success power of persistence worked for the author. How the plagues were blessings in disguise. How to handle it when things get worse. The prospering power of letting go graciously. How he lost a job but gained a position. What to do when bondage tries to recapture you. Why her demonstration faded. How to keep your good by holding your peace. How he avoided a lawsuit by keeping quiet. How to cross your Red Sea. How a dying woman recovered. How $400 came to a housewife. How doing the fearless thing brought new prosperity to a church. How doing the fearless thing worked for the author. How a professor crossed his Red Sea and prospered by giving thanks. How to seal your good. A meditation to help you use the prosperity law of fearlessness.

4. HOW TO GATHER YOUR PROSPEROUS MANNA 71

Why gathering manna was necessary. The purpose of a financial wilderness. The lavish abundance that awaited them in the Promised Land. How a businessman prospered in his financial wilderness. Your initiation into prosperity's deeper levels. How a maid became a prosperous shopowner and regained her health. How an officer multiplied food for his soldiers. How she stretched the food on hand. How a merchant gathered manna. How a college student gathered manna. How a young couple gathered manna. How an ill, hungry woman gathered manna through picturing. How manna has appeared to prosper the author. When she blessed another's prosperity, she also received new supply. How $2,000 came to them to pay their debts. How he sold his car at the last minute. How to get out of a financial wilderness forever. A prosperity meditation for gathering your manna.

5. Your Secret Weapons For Prosperity 94

Your first secret weapon for prosperity. How this prosperity secret has worked for the author. Your second secret weapon for prosperity. How you can use this secret weapon. The success power of prayer partners. How an English shopkeeper met the mortgage payment. How this secret weapon cured a hopeless health prob, lem. How she freed her father from prison. How a mother healed her son of drinking. How he was healed of mistreating an employee. How she brought about reconciliation of two friends. Your third secret weapon for prosperity. How to resolve hard conditions in your life. How a kindergarten teacher improved her world with words. How a businesswoman moved into a better job. How to speak to your rock. How a landlord rented rooms successfully. How a teenager made new friends. Rename your difficulties. How a wife saved her marriage with words. How to clear rocky conditions out of your life. A meditation for invoking your secret weapons for prosperity.

6. The Prosperity Commandments 118

The first prosperity commandment. How a schoolteacher became wealthy. The second prosperity commandment. How a famous golfer succeeded. The third prosperity commandment. How he became a famous playwright. The fourth prosperity commandment. The fifth prosperity commandment. How a mother helped her troubled teenage daughter. The sixth prosperity commandment. How accountant helped everyone in his office. The seventh prosperity commandment. How a businessman got a car but with strings attached and learned a valuable lesson. The eighth prosperity commandment. How a chronic illness was finally healed. The ninth prosperity commandment. How you can keep this prosperity commandment. The tenth prosperity commandment. How to claim your good instead of coveting someone else's good.

7. The Prosperity Law of Opulence 142

Why opulence is necessary to you. How to expand your opulence consciousness. The surprise inheritance. Do's and don'ts of opulent thinking. How she got her husband back. How she was healed

of arthritis. How your good can arrive ten times quicker. How two
men became millionaires. From poverty to a $13 million dollar
income. How they went from rags to riches. How to invoke the
law of opulence through giving properly. Why the world loves
prosperous spiritual workers. Why the priests were millionaires.
How she received $250. How a retired person received $100. They
had to be restrained from giving!

8. THE MIRACLE LAW OF PROSPERITY 165

How thanksgiving put food on the table and provided quick
cash. How thanksgiving opened the way to pay his bills. How a
nurse activated her prosperity quickly. The "thank you box" method. How sixteen requests were fulfilled through the "thank you
box" method. How the "thank you box" method worked for the
author. How a marriage is restored and a good job obtained.
Thanksgiving should take a definite financial form. How you can
receive vast benefits. A meditation that can produce prosperity
miracles for you!

9. THE PROSPERITY LAW OF PREPARATION 181

How Moses used the law of preparation. How you can use the
prosperity law of preparation. How he prepared for a new career
mentally first. How a wife's preparation helped her husband become a millionaire. How a jobless man prepared to become a millionaire. How to draw your good out of the invisible. How she
married a popular bachelor. How to make a move toward the
prosperity you want. How the author visited a certain area after
preparing to do so. How a businessman prepared for a new wardrobe and got it. How deliberate preparation brought her a home.
Do something to show you expect results. Moses' prosperity warning. How a schoolteacher made, then lost, a fortune. Blessings or
curses—it's up to you. Why he lost a fortune. How to avoid curses
and claim blessings. A meditation to help you invoke the prosperity law of preparation.

10. THE PROSPERITY LAW OF COMPLETION 201

Why Joshua and Caleb had been restrained. Speak the word of completion. How the word of completion brought change of jobs. An occult formula for results. How they prospered when things got tight financially. How a doctor manifested supply. How to get through a transition period. How a college student proved this. Why you must also let go the pleasant cycles. How the act of blessing brings completion. How she went from caretaker to a manager's job. Find a point of agreement. Dramatic changes come anyway. Your success formula for completion.

IN CONCLUSION: YOUR PROSPERITY CHARGE 218
How to Enter Your Promised Land of Abundance

YOUR PROSPERITY IS UNLIMITED!

A SPECIAL MESSAGE FROM THE AUTHOR

This book relates some amazing stories of how those involved experienced unlimited prosperity:

A Los Angeles businessman had lost a fortune, but made it again. This time he kept it because he had learned how to do so from within out. A sickly businessman was first healed. By using the same success method that healed him, he made a fortune. He continues to enjoy his enormous wealth and good health until this day.

A discouraged widow learned one of the secret success methods described in this book and quietly used it. She soon married into one of the most famous super-rich families in America! She now travels in international society and enjoys a fabulous life. Another widow received a large gift of money. A prominent minister went from a $6500 to a $30,000 annual income. After eleven years' separation, a housewife was reunited with her husband, and they are now busy "living happily ever after."

1

A businessman lost a job, but gained a position. Another businessman learned what to do to avoid a costly lawsuit. A dying woman recovered. A whining maid became a radiant, prosperous shopkeeper. $2000 came to one couple with which to pay off their debts.

In the pages of this book, you will learn how these people accomplished such prosperous results, and how you can too.

"PROSPERITY UNLIMITED" BEGAN DURING A RECESSION

What is prosperity? It is not limited to any one phase of your life. Prosperity includes your increased peace, health and plenty. It is an experience in perpetual growth which leads to constant expansion of your world in both inner and outer ways. That expansion leads to your *"Prosperity Unlimited"*! That is what this book is all about.

On a sunny afternoon in 1958, from my "gold dust study" in an old Southern mansion (the building in which I worked) in Birmingham, Alabama, I wrote my first prosperity article. It described a prosperity class I had conducted during the recession of 1958, and it related the amazing results of those who had attended.

There had been job promotions, raises in pay, increased business orders, new customers and clients, bills collected, even the winning of an all-expense-paid trip abroad — in the midst of a recessional atmosphere of bread lines, unemployment, and "hard-times" talk. Physical healings, the gift of a financial inheritance, new marriages, and other worthwhile "fringe benefits" had also resulted for those who had attended that prosperity class.

In 1959, my article describing the results of that prosperity class was published in a magazine for business people. It brought so many responses that the editor asked me to continue researching and writing on the subject of prosperity and success.

I did, and my life hasn't been the same since! Neither will yours—as you begin to use the fascinating laws of prosperity described in this book—those first used by the millionaire Moses.

HOW THE AUTHOR PROSPERED

You probably have regarded a millionaire as one who has a million dollars or more, but in its root the word "millionaire" means "abundance and happiness." Increased health, wealth, happiness and spiritual understanding are *all* possible when you begin to use the prosperity secrets described in this book.

At the time I so innocently wrote that first prosperity article in 1958, I was an unknown writer and a nondenominational minister with a congregation numbering less than one hundred people. Though I was working around the clock, my income was still at a poverty level. I had been widowed, and my growing son and I were living in the one room that was provided for us by the church I then served. To say that I was struggling to expand my thinking and my world would be putting it mildly.

As I wrote that prosperity article, observed its publication, and started dwelling upon the possibility of unlimited prosperity for myself and for others, good things began to happen.

The church's income increased and the congregation grew. My son and I moved out of that one room into a lovely new church manse. We were able to employ a house-keeper to take care of us, and to purchase some beautiful furnishings for our new abode.

Since that time, my world has continued to expand. I moved on, first to Texas, then a decade later to the meta-physical atmosphere of Southern California. I have writ-ten a number of best selling books including the popular *Dynamic Laws of Prosperity*[1] which continues to reach thousands in a paperback edition. I have lectured extensive-ly and have appeared from coast to coast on television and on radio news shows to talk about the power of prosperous thinking. With the help of the appreciative readers of my books, I have founded three new nondenominational churches from "financial scratch."

My income has improved. This has made it possible to expand my staff and to reduce the heavy burden of the per-sonal work load which I carried alone for so many years.

I am now grateful to be living in the beautiful Palm Desert-Palm Springs area, long called "the playground of the rich." I reside in a celebrity neighborhood where many famous show-business personalities have owned homes. I now live and work in an atmosphere of lush tropical beauty in this desert retreat. Such surroundings are a vast inspira-

---

1. Catherine Ponder, *The Dynamic Laws of Prosperity* (Marina del Rey, CA: DeVorss & Co., 1983).

tion to me as I continue to do research and to write about the power of prosperous thinking.

Although there has been no flash flood of supply for me, gradually as I have expanded my thinking and expectations, so has my world been enriched. Since success is progressive, there is much greater abundance and happiness still to come on all levels of my life as I persist in using the prosperity principles described in this book.

As you also learn and apply the prosperity secrets of the millionaire Moses, I trust that similar blessings—and many, many more—shall come to you!

HOW THIS BOOK CAN PROSPER YOU

The purpose of this book is to remind you of what you may already know: That prosperity is your heritage. Every normal person is vitally interested in the subject of prosperity.

Indeed, *an expanded prosperity consciousness is a necessity in this age of increasing economic demands. Rising prices, "inflationary recessions," and uncertain political and economic world conditions are all indications that we must raise and expand our consciousness to a new level of universal supply.*

Through using the prosperity laws described in this book, you can deliberately get into a universal prosperity vibration, and begin to experience more successful results in every phase of your life. *Whatever you most need next in your life can open to you, as you open your mind to the prosperity secrets of the millionaire Moses!*

To develop a prosperity consciousness—and all the vast benefits that go with it—is easier than you may have realized. Why? Because there are those who traveled the path before you many centuries ago who knew, taught, and practiced the universal laws of unlimited prosperity. As you apply the simple principles they used, there will be nothing mysterious or haphazard about it. Your prosperity will be assured.

MEET THE MILLIONAIRE MOSES

During that recessional period in 1958, I turned to the Bible for prosperous guidance. I quickly discovered that the Bible is the greatest textbook on prosperity that has ever been written! It is "loaded" with millionaires.

In fact, many of our modern millionaires could hardly afford the affluent life style of the millionaires of the Bible, with their vast flocks, huge land holdings, large families, and unlimited staff of servants. It was a gracious, generous, leisurely way of life that might be difficult even for a Rockefeller to maintain at today's prices. The frantic, hard-work, competitive consciousness of twentieth-century man can hardly conceive that life style. Yet the abundant prosperity consciousness of the millionaires of the Bible is still available to us today.

In the decades that have followed that discovery in 1958, I have been busy researching the prosperity secrets of the millionaires of the Bible, and have begun writing a series of books about them. The first book in the series was *The*

Millionaires of Genesis.[2] That book included a description of the life of Joseph, the displaced Hebrew who became the billionaire Prime Minister of Egypt. This book continues the prosperity story of the Hebrews, how they dramatically escaped Egyptian bondage, how they survived and even prospered in the wilderness, and how they progressed to the edge of their long-awaited Promised Land.

In the pages of this book, you will meet one of the most prominent millionaires of the Old Testament, Moses, whom I like to think of as "Mr. Prosperity," or "Mr. Success." Both Christians and Jews have long realized he was one of the most outstanding leaders of all times. His early background in Egypt exposed him to their immense material wealth and all of its benefits. He was reared a millionaire at the court of King Pharaoh. There he also was given secret instruction on the inner laws of prosperity and how to use them.

Later he became a master teacher of prosperity in the Old Testament. No other group of people has ever been able to surpass the vast wealth that came to his followers over the centuries as they used the prosperity principles which he laid down under divine guidance for them. *Only a mystic's knowledge of the inner laws of prosperity, which Moses first learned in Egypt, and later shared with the Hebrews, could have assured any group of such astounding wealth over the centuries. Theirs was far more than a material wealth; theirs was a mystical wealth.* That is why it has grown and expanded for them over the centuries, rather than diminished.

---

2. Catherine Ponder, *The Millionaires of Genesis* (Marina del Rey, Calif.: DeVorss & Co., 1976).

As you begin to use the same universal prosperity laws Moses used and taught, you will find yourself being freed from the bondage of limited thinking and limited living. You, too, will discover your own *"Prosperity Unlimited"* and then expand into your Promised Land of increasing abundance!

A PROSPERITY INVITATION TO YOU

I invite you to begin right now to expand and to enrich your world by meditating often upon that thought I so innocently first used during that recession in 1958, and which I have continued to use over the years: *"My prosperity is unlimited. My success is unlimited now."*

I also invite you to turn quickly to the following pages and meet the millionaire Moses. As you do so, I predict that his influence upon your life will be as unforgettable as it has been upon mine.

I shall look forward to a letter from you, describing the prosperous results that come to you as you study his prosperity secrets contained in this book, and freely apply them in your life.

CATHERINE PONDER

P.O. Drawer 1278
Palm Desert, California 92261
U.S.A.

PROSPERITY IN THREE PARTS FOR YOU

— Chapter 1 —

A cartoon showed a concerned businessman studying the financial page of the newspaper. He grumbled to his wife, "I cannot tell from these stock reports whether we are still 'lousy rich' or merely 'rich.'"

As you study the prosperity secrets of the millionaire Moses, I trust they will help you feel and become not merely "rich" but "lousy rich" as did the descendants of Moses!

THE MILLIONAIRE MOSES

A "millionaire" is usually considered to be one who is worth a million dollars or more. In its root the word "millionaire" also means "abundance and happiness." Moses met both of these definitions because he became a millionaire both mentally and financially. He was a millionaire of the first order because he also taught his followers the secret of true prosperity: how to prosper from the inside out.

9

At the court of Pharaoh, Moses' exposure to the vast abundance of Egypt—the wealthiest civilization of ancient times—helped to prepare him inwardly for the great work that lay ahead: That of leading the enslaved Hebrews out of financial bondage to the Egyptians, through a barren wilderness where they learned how to trust God one day at a time for their supply, to the edge of their own prosperous Promised Land in which they were to become very rich.

PROSPERITY IN THE FIRST PERIOD

There is a perennial charm about the picture of the infant, Moses, floating along the Nile River in thriving, prosperous Egypt. There he was rescued by a beautiful princess. That princess, who became his adopted mother, was among the richest women of the ancient world because she was the daughter of the billionaire, King Pharaoh.

Moses was reared a millionaire at the court of King Pharaoh, where he was exposed to immense material wealth and all of its vast benefits. Young Moses was very popular at court as he went about in fine garments. He was provided a royal education, and he developed the manners and bearing of the aristocratic Royal Family. As a member of the powerful Pharaoh's family, Moses learned how to be a "somebody." He developed self-confidence, a trained mind, and vast technical knowledge. These assets were to serve him well later in his role as prosperous leader of the Hebrew people.

Whether Moses ever served as a priest in the mystical temples of Egypt has been debated. But it is interesting to note that the word "Moses" in an esoteric Egyptian sense meant "one who has been admitted into the mystery schools of wisdom." Moses later taught the Jews a powerful success philosophy, which some historians feel contained the secret principles of Egyptian esotericism. There are those who claim that when Moses set up the twelve tribes of Israel, he established a secret school of wisdom in the midst of them called "the tabernacle mysteries."

Legend also states that when Moses established his mystery school, he gave a few chosen initiates certain oral teachings, which were never written, but were passed on from one generation to the next by word of mouth. That instruction was in the form of philosophical keys based upon metaphysical interpretation, some of which are still known and taught today. The most obvious prosperity principles that Moses used are found in this book. Of course, the first five books of the Bible, attributed to Moses' authorship, contain even more in both literal and allegorical form.

Of one thing we can be sure: Moses was given secret instruction on the inner laws of prosperity and how to use them. As an Egyptian prince, Moses was instructed in all the secrets of the Egyptian priesthood, which included instruction in metaphysics, and instruction in the secret teaching that "substance" was the key to all wealth. Earlier, the Bible's first millionaire, Abraham, had learned this same prosperity secret from the wealthy Babylonians. When Abraham passed it on to his followers, they too became millionaires. (See my book *The Millionaires of Genesis, Their Prosperity Secrets for You.*[1])

---

1. Catherine Ponder, *The Millionaires of Genesis* (Marina del Rey, Calif.: DeVorss & Co., 1976).

This prosperity secret—that "substance" is the basis of all wealth—which Moses learned from the Egyptians was powerful enough to help him free the Hebrews from the feared, materialistic Pharaoh. As he taught them how to continue to dwell upon "substance" as the basis of their supply, they were able to survive in the barren wilderness for forty years, and to travel to the edge of their fabled Promised Land in which they were to enjoy unparalleled wealth! Not only was Moses a millionaire, he became an excellent prosperity teacher whose success philosophy influenced many generations of future millionaires, bringing them astounding wealth. And that was a prosperity achievement that has not been surpassed in the history of mankind!

HOW MOSES' EGYPTIAN EXPERIENCE
CAN PROSPER YOU

The story of Moses is described in the Book of Exodus. The word "Exodus" means "a way out of trouble." Just as Exodus was a book of the Law, so this book describes the universal laws that can show you the way out of trouble and limitation, beginning with the three periods of Moses' life which give us clues to his success:

The *first* period in Moses life spent in Egypt, was a time of mental and intellectual development. People who only learn *about* life from a mental and intellectual standpoint often make the mistake that Moses made during this period. They try to use their knowledge to force their good. Like Moses, they get a negative reaction. Moses had to escape from Egypt because he killed an Egyptian.

The Egyptian he killed symbolizes any form of limitation in your life, or any problem, which you try to kill out. Instead of getting free from the problem, your reaction can bring more problems to you. *Moses had not yet learned that he could not force people and conditions to do what he wanted.* He had not realized there was a higher and better way.

Most of us, when first instructed in the power of thought, are like Moses. We try to use our new-found power to force other people to do as we wish. If so, we get a negative reaction.

However, like Moses, when you blunder in this way, you can still draw the good out of apparent negative experiences! For this purpose declare: *"Only good shall come from this."*

During the *first* period of Moses' life he was exposed to the material consciousness of immense wealth that was enjoyed by King Pharaoh and the affluent Egyptians. However, it was during this same period that he learned the inner laws of prosperity, and how to create his prosperity mentally first, while attending the wisdom schools of Egypt.

Having an appreciation of *outer* material wealth, and a knowledge of the *inner* creative methods of wealth, were the two keys that gave him a balanced prosperity consciousness. This combined knowledge made him the master teacher of prosperity of the Old Testament.

Many people gain one or the other. They have either: (1) an appreciation of visible wealth, but are unaware of its true metaphysical source; or (2) knowledge of the source of metaphysical prosperity, but are not appreciative enough of it in visible, material form. *The greatness of Moses lay in his ability to appreciate both sides of prosperity: The physical and the metaphysical.* This he had learned from his life in Egypt. Thus, this *first* period of his life was very important as it provided a foundation for all that followed.

PROSPERITY IN THE SECOND PERIOD

During the *second* phase of Moses' life, after killing the Egyptian, Moses escaped into the Midian Desert where he spent the next forty years of his life. This became a time of mental reflection and inner growth.

Upon his arrival in the Midian Desert, Moses met with good fortune. There at a rare and precious well of water, he got acquainted with the family of the prosperous Jethro, who was a successful shepherd and wealthy trader. Jethro was a person of great importance as Chief Priest of the tribe. His fine manners and generous hospitality to Moses indicated that he was "a highborn Arab." When Moses married Jethro's daughter, he "married well" into Midianite aristocracy.

The peace of mind, emotional stability, and maturity Moses gained during this period was to serve him well in his future prosperity mission.

WHAT MOSES' MIDIAN DESERT EXPERIENCES
MEAN TO YOU

In the Midian Desert, Moses had time to think, meditate, and turn within to develop his deeper powers. The word

"Midian" means "strife and contention." Moses needed this quiet period to overcome strife and contention within himself. He realized that instead of trying to straighten out other people, he would do well to straighten out his own thoughts and feelings. This was a time for discipline of his personal will.

When you first learn about the power of your thoughts, as did Moses during the first period of his life spent in Egypt, you may be inclined to try to use mind power to mentally force your will on others. Instead, you need to turn within and overcome the strife and contention within your own thoughts and feelings. When you have disciplined your personal will, you are then ready for what comes next in your growth.

Through this long period of solitude Moses gained inner strength. The exacting disciplines of self-unfoldment, which were to continue throughout his life, had begun. Only through solitude, after Moses had gained control of his personal will and had become peaceful within, did he get ready for the next step in his expanded good.

One day, while Moses was keeping Jethro's flock near Mount Horeb, Jehovah appeared to him in the bush that burned but was not consumed. The word "Horeb" means "solitude."

The burning bush symbolizes your burning intuition—that "still small voice" of wisdom within you—that begins to come alive in this second phase of the development of your prosperity consciousness. Once your intuitive nature comes alive, it is like that burning bush that cannot be consumed or put out. You will hear it offering you guidance and wisdom again and again.

As he stood looking at the bush, Moses was told by Jehovah to take off his shoes because he was on holy ground. The feet symbolize understanding. Taking off his shoes symbolized freeing his thinking from limited ideas—deliberately letting them go in order to expand his thinking and his world. When you are trying to do this declare often: *"My life (health, wealth, happiness) cannot be limited. I am now freed from all limitation. I now move forward into my expanded good, divinely directed and lavishly prospered. All things conform to the right thing for me now quickly and in peace."*

As you learn to listen to the intuitive ideas that well up within you in your times of solitude, you will always be guided into that which is best for you. There is nothing too great for you to accomplish as you follow your intuitive leads. Never argue with a hunch. Follow it without apology to anyone. It can lead you straight into your Promised Land of Abundance!

HOW INTUITION PROSPERED A BUSINESSMAN

A businessman in Los Angeles told me that for years he suppressed his intuition. He had not realized it was a part of his God-nature and that he should listen to it. As he followed the logical advice of others, everything went wrong in his life. He made a lot of money, then he lost it. Bad health and a hectic family life followed.

At this low point in his life, he read my book, *The Dynamic Laws of Prosperity*,[2] which explained that the per-

---

2. Catherine Ponder, *The Dynamic Laws of Prosperity* (Marina del Rey, CA: DeVorss & Co., rev. ed. 1983).

sistent hunches he had often felt well up within him were a part of his indwelling God-nature. They were his genius powers for prosperity and he should act upon them instead of suppressing them.

When this businessman began to follow his hunches, it was like setting his feet on a magic path of plenty. Everything improved and straightened out in his life. He said to me, "For the first time in my life, I am really living. Life is exciting and satisfying when I dare to follow my intuitive leads. They have already led me into greater abundance."

When there is a persistent prompting to act, that prompting is always accompanied by the power to produce results, so follow it.

Through following your intuitive hunches, you can solve problems that you will never solve in any other way! The more you turn within for guidance—rather than without—the more sensitive you will become to "the still small voice" and the more your intuition will deliver you out of the bondage of limited living into your expanded good.

HOW MOSES' INTUITION PROSPERED
TWO MILLION PEOPLE

It was during this *second* period of Moses' life that Jehovah told him he was to deliver the enslaved Israelites from Egyptian bondage. At first Moses doubted his ability to perform such a gigantic task, but once he was assured by Jehovah that he would be well able to do it, he did not argue, reason or analyze. He set out on his prosperity mission promptly. From his quiet years in the Midianite Desert, he had gained the inner strength needed to appear before the powerful billionaire, King Pharaoh, and dare to persist in demanding, "Let my people go." (Exodus 5:1, 7:16)

Because he followed his intuitive guidance promptly, Moses was able to deliver what may have been as many as two million people out of the clutches of the most powerful monarch of that age. And he did it through intuition.

Your intuition will do for you what nothing else can! The more you become aware of the mind powers within you through practice of quietness and meditation, the more intuitive you will become, and the more your intuition will deliver you out of bondage to limited living. Your intuition is your genius power for success.

MOSES' MISSION WAS TO REVEAL
YOUR DIVINE NATURE

One of the missions of Moses was to show the Children of Israel that they had a divine nature within them called the *"I AM"* which would lead them out of bondage.

A sure way to develop your genius power of intuition is to dwell often in your meditations upon your own divine *"I AM"* power. Then release that divine power through speaking forth *"I AM"* statements.

When Jehovah spoke to Moses through the burning bush experience, He told Moses that the *universal* God power, which would help him, was named *"I AM THAT I AM."* The *indwelling* God power, which would help him, was named *"I AM."* (Exodus 3:14)

The term *"I AM"* was one that was well known to the ancient people. They regarded it as a term of great power. Moses had been familiar from childhood with the power found in the words *"I AM"* because those words appeared on the walls of every Egyptian temple. After Jehovah's instruction to Moses, the Hebrews used the term *"I AM"* so much that they became known as "the people of the *I AM.*" They considered the term *"I AM"* the lost word of power which, when released in meditation and through spoken decrees, could perform miracles in an instant.

HOW TO USE YOUR ROD OF POWER SUCCESSFULLY

When Moses doubted his ability to get his followers out of the clutches of the mighty Pharaoh, Jehovah gave him a rod to help him. When Moses lifted the rod, it brought blessings. When he lowered it, the rod brought curses. Your *"I AM"* is your rod of power.

Your *"I AM"* power releases your divine nature to work miracles for you, too! There are strange powers lying dormant within that Name. All that you dream of as desirable for you can be released through affirming *"I AM"* because *"I AM"* is the name of the God power within you. Meditation upon that Name will give you clairvoyant powers as it reveals to you all that you need to know.

Every time you say, "I am sick," "I am weak," or "I am discouraged," you are speaking God's name falsely and you will get a false result. The *"I AM"* nature of God within you cannot be sick or discouraged because it is filled with life, power, unlimited good. *"I AM"* spoken upward toward increased good causes it to outpicture in your life.

Do you doubt that such power can be released through speaking that Name? Go alone, close your eyes, and speak over and over the words "*I AM.*" Soon you will feel your whole being filled with a sense of power you had not previously known. *Just try for one week always saying the words "I AM" upward toward the good and see what the results will be!*

HOW TO BRING VAST IMPROVEMENT INTO YOUR LIFE

Many people have witnessed vast improvement in their lives by following this simple practice:

On retiring at night, just before sleeping, they say: "*I am health, strength, peace, happiness, and prosperity. I am strong, well, vital. I am beautiful, peaceful, poised. I am eternally youthful. I am happy and free.*"

Others have worked out their problems from that of overcoming lifelong poverty to the healing of physical disorders by this simple process. One metaphysician has predicted that the day will come when people everywhere will know about their "*I AM*" power for success. They will stop saying "I am sick" and they will be healed by using their "*I AM*" power in a positive way.

There once was a man who proved this. His diseased condition had been diagnosed as incurable. He kept affirming "*I praise God that I am healed now*" so long that it happened.

Everytime you use your "*I AM*" power downward, you shorten your life. But when you say, "*I am one with God and his goodness,"* you improve your life. Everytime you go forth using the name *"I AM"* upward, it opens doors, dissolves obstacles, and prepares the way for you. When you use the term *"I AM"* upward, you get blessings, whereas when you use it negatively you get problems.

Say to your problems: *"I AM hath sent me."* This opens the way to surmount all difficulties. When you become aware of other people's problems, you can release a universal power for good by declaring for them *"I AM THAT I AM* is mightily at work for you now!"*

A lady kept trying to solve an apparently hopeless problem. Nothing worked out right until she began to deliberately say: *"With God's help, I am going to make it."* Suddenly the tide turned and everything came her way.

Everytime you say *"I AM"* you have gripped a handle of power. You make your destiny by the things which you attach to the words *"I AM."* The term *"I AM"* has been called "the song of Moses" because it was considered his secret text for success. It can become your song for success too! (See chapter on the *"I AM"* in my book, *The Dynamic Laws of Healing.*[3])

HOW THEY BECAME MILLIONAIRES

I have known of two people who became millionaires after they began daily to meditate upon and affirm *"I AM"* statements. One was a sickly businessman who first was

3. Catherine Ponder, *The Dynamic Laws of Healing* (Marina del Rey, Calif.: DeVorss & Co., rev. ed. 1985).

healed by calling on the name *"I AM."* As he continued to call on that name, he made a fortune in the stock market. He has enjoyed his enormous wealth for several decades, and continues in good health.

The second person was a discouraged widow. As she began to call on the name *"I AM,"* she married into one of the most famous super-rich families in America. She now travels in international society and enjoys a fabulous life.

PROSPERITY IN THE THIRD PERIOD

The *third* period of Moses' life was spent in the wilderness, molding the unruly Hebrew slaves into a self-sufficient and prosperous nation. That he had learned the inner prosperity laws well is shown in the way he was able to provide food and water for such a large company in that barren place. To those hungry, thirsty people, it was a prosperity miracle of millionaire proportions!

That Moses had developed an appreciation of the prospering power of literal wealth and beauty while still at the court of Egypt is shown in this last period of his life, when he erected the lavish tabernacle in which the Hebrews worshipped.

The solid gold candlesticks that were used were worth at least $25,000. The amount of gold, silver and brass used in constructing the moveable sanctuary amounted to more than $400,000 — pre-inflation prices. The Hebrews had brought these valuable portable possessions with them from Egypt. Before their departure, they had asked for and re-

ceived presents from their Egyptian neighbors. (Exodus
11:2; 12:35, 36) Such exchange was considered a diplo-
matic courtesy. Our modern churches should be like the
elegant tabernacle of the Hebrews: the most beautiful,
prosperous, cared-for buildings in the community. One of
the highest forms of worship is art.

Moses' belief in the importance of wearing beautiful clothing is indicated in the bejeweled garments he ordered de-
signed for the first High Priest of Israel. These clothes were
described as "garments for glory and beauty." (Exodus
28:2) These were made of fine linen in brilliant colors set
in gold, worn with emeralds, diamonds and other precious
stones. They were made only by "skillful workmen," who
would be equivalent to our modern designers and tailors.
(Exodus 28:6)

Moses taught the once-unruly Hebrews to develop such
a lavish prosperity consciousness, right in the midst of that
barren wilderness, that they had "to be restrained from giving" for the construction of the new tabernacle because
they "gave too much." (Exodus 36:6, 7) Never in the history of church building programs has that happened—
before or since!

Before his transition, Moses ascended Mount Nebo where
he viewed with satisfaction the magnificent panorama of
the rich Promised Land, which had been described earlier
as "flowing with milk and honey." (Exodus 3:8, 17; 33:3)
Viewing it from afar, Moses knew that his prosperity mission was accomplished.

When Moses brought his followers to the edge of the
Promised Land, he had brought them to the edge of the
Land of Canaan. The word "Canaan" symbolizes "realm of

substance." Through the use of the prosperity laws he laid down for his followers, Moses had led them metaphysically into an understanding of the realm of substance, which was to be the key to their future super-wealth.

Because of his understanding of the nature of substance as the foundation of everything, Moses' appearance at the age of 120 was one of perpetual youth—a true manifestation of radiant substance. He was the only person in the Bible to have God as his undertaker. (Deuteronomy 34:6) Later Jesus proudly said, "Moses wrote of me." (John 5:46) Like Jesus, Moses also reappeared after death. (Matthew 17:3) (Acts 1:3) It is no wonder that in this century, the illustrious David Livingston called Moses his favorite Bible hero.

HOW MOSES' WILDERNESS EXPERIENCE
   ## CAN PROSPER YOU

This *third* or last forty-year period of Moses' life, spent in the wilderness, was a time of ups and downs for the Hebrews.

Sometimes they were happy to have been delivered from Egyptian bondage. At other times, they criticized Moses severely for having brought them into the desolate wilderness. *Because of their "murmurings" they remained in the wilderness for forty years.* (Numbers 14:26-30) *They could have gotten into their Promised Land much sooner had they not criticized Moses and murmured against their wilderness experiences.*

This *third* phase of Moses' life symbolizes what usually happens to you as you begin to develop your mind powers:

1. You learn about the power of thought intellectually and perhaps rush forth to use it on others, or to kill out your problems with it. If so, you find out quickly that such mental force brings a negative reaction.

2. This causes you to turn within to begin overcoming the strife and contention within your own thoughts and feelings. As you do so, your intuitive powers come alive. When you follow your intuitive hunches, they lead you out of bondage and limitation.

3. Then you begin to have your "ups and downs" in the use of mind power and in the use of your genius power of intuition. How should you meet your "up and down" periods successfully? If you fight the new experiences that may seem to be wilderness periods, you will just remain in those experiences that much longer. If you do not resist those "up and down" periods, but bless them as times of growth, you get through them much quicker and arrive safely in your Promised Land. This happens as you stabilize your prosperity consciousness through your persistent use of the inner laws of prosperity.

THE PROSPERITY MISSION OF MOSES

The mission of Moses has been described as that of emancipator of his people from their awful Egyptian bondage. He was that, but much more.

The mission of Moses was a prosperity mission. The Hebrews had gone to Egypt because of their desire for prosperity during the seven-year famine in the time when their famous kinsman, Joseph, was Prime Minister of Egypt.

Not only did Joseph save them from starvation, he arranged for them to remain in Egypt where they lived in prosperous comfort. As long as the popular Joseph remained in power, his kinsmen were welcomed in Egypt. At his passing, the Egyptians began to resent the Hebrews, and to regard them as "gold diggers." The humiliation of Egyptian slavery and bondage followed.

The mission of Moses was to help the Hebrews realize that God was the source of their supply—not the Egyptians. His mission was to help them realize that they did not have to remain in cruel financial bondage to a hard taskmaster in order to be prospered, and to show them that they could enjoy prosperous living in their own Promised Land, which was flowing with abundance.

Through use of certain mental laws, Moses led the Hebrews out of Egyptian bondage. He then helped them prove that God could supply their needs, one day at a time, as manna from heaven and as water from the rock. In spite of his proof to them that God was an all-providing Father, they were not satisfied. Even though they had been slaves in Egypt, at least they hade been assured of a reasonable degree of prosperity, they reasoned.

Like many people today, the critical Hebrews were willing to settle for a compromise with the lesser blessings in life, rather than to exert faith in God as their supply, which could lead them into unlimited abundance. When the Hebrews criticized and opposed Moses in the wilderness, he turned to God and asked for guidance in leading these rebellious people to the edge of the Promised Land. Moses was able to do this through use of definite prosperity laws, which you can use to work your way out of financial limitation, so that you arrive in your Promised Land of abundance too!

YOUR PROSPERITY MISSION

Like the Hebrews in Egypt, you have a material understanding of prosperity when you feel that people and conditions control your good. When you begin to realize there are mind powers within you which can free you from depending on others for your supply, you may become restless. You will want freedom to prosper through use of your inner powers.

As you use "the dynamic laws of prosperity" and that freedom comes, you suddenly find you are on your own. It can be a challenge to try to prosper through use of your inner powers. As you go from the competitive and material methods of demonstrating prosperity — symbolized by the Hebrews enslaved in Egypt—to a creative inner level of prosperity—symbolized by the Hebrews freed in the wilderness—you too may have your "ups and downs." As you first begin to use the inner laws of prosperity, you may even look back upon your former methods of supply, reasoning that half a loaf was better than none.

I vividly recall my departure from a material, outer consciousness of supply. It took place twenty years ago when I left my job in the business world in North Carolina, where

I had looked to my employer for a weekly pay check. With only $30 in my pocket, I arrived as a minister-in-training in Alabama, where I would have to look to God for guidance and supply one day at a time, since there would be no guaranteed income. Momentarily, I looked back upon the former methods of supply I had used in the business world, wondering if half a loaf wasn't better than none. But as I researched and began to use "the dynamic laws of prosperity," a whole new method of being supplied from within unfolded gradually, so that my needs were quietly met in ways I could not have foreseen.

Later when I founded a church in Texas from financial scratch, I had a further opportunity to prove the inner methods of supply. I recall sitting in the huge, empty, football stadium at the University of Texas—located near my apartment—where I often said prosperity affirmations outloud. (Not only did I go there for the privacy factor. Since it is one of the wealthiest universities in the world, I reasoned that declaring prosperity statements on its grounds might help me become attuned to a similar prosperity consciousness.) I made wheels of fortune picturing the supply needed for that new church, and for me personally. I vowed to begin tithing two-tenths of my gross income during that period, rather than only one-tenth as in the past.

I now realize that lean period was an "initiation in substance," or an experience in moving out of Egyptian bondage into a financial wilderness. There I was learning how to gain "an inner hold" on substance, and this knowledge was to lead me into my Promised Land. By the time I had completed my work with the founding of that church, I felt strong enough in my understanding of the inner laws of prosperity—and in having gained "an inner hold" on substance—to try it all over again, and found a second church from financial scratch. This time it was much easier, and the supply was provided much quicker. By the time I founded a third ministry in California, I felt that I had moved out of a financial wilderness, and was well on the way into my Promised Land of an enduring supply.

I would not care to repeat my "initiation in substance" experiences which have taken place over this twenty-year period. But I no longer fear lack, because I have learned (as did the Hebrews in their wilderness experiences) that the inner realm of prosperity is the only one upon which we can truly depend for our supply. People in all walks of life have related to me similar experiences of being initiated into prosperity's deeper levels of supply.

Going from a material, outer consciousness of prosperity to a creative, inner one is the universal experience of all evolving souls. Abraham, Isaac, Jacob and Joseph experienced it (as described in detail in my book, *The Millionaires of Genesis*), and you probably will too, as you expand your prosperity consciousness.

WHY SOME NEVER GOT INTO THE PROMISED LAND

The gripers never got into the Promised Land. They died in the wilderness. Only those who could mentally accept their Promised Land ever entered it.

If you do not fight your wilderness experiences, but learn from them, and if you grow through them by persistent use of the inner laws of prosperity, you will not bog down in failure, but you will arrive in your Promised Land of abundance as soon as you are ready for it!

In those "up and down" periods when you are inclined to doubt this, you can stir up your *"I AM"* power for success by declaring often, *"I am rich, well and happy, and every phase of my life is in divine order now."*

Then meditate often upon the prosperity promise of Jehovah to the Children of Israel, which was destined to make them millionaires:

> "I have seen the affliction of my people that are in Egypt, and have heard their cry . . . and I am come down to deliver them out of the hand of the Egyptians. I am come . . . to bring them up out of that land unto a good land and a large, unto a land flowing with milk and honey."
>
> (Exodus 3:7, 8)

This is your promise of abundance too!

SUMMARY

1. The word "millionaire" in its root means "abundance and happiness." Moses became a millionaire both mentally and financially. He also taught his followers the secret of true prosperity.

2. The *first* period of Moses' life was one of mental and intellectual development at the court of Pharaoh, where he was surrounded by lavish abundance and lived as a young millionaire. According to legend, he attended a wisdom school during this period where he learned the inner laws of prosperity, too. The greatness of Moses lay in his ability to appreciate both sides of prosperity: the physical and the metaphysical, as learned during this *first* period of his life spent in Egypt. This combined knowledge gave him a balanced prosperity consciousness which later made him the master teacher of prosperity of the Old Testament.

3. The *second* period of Moses' life, spent in the Midian Desert, was a time of mental reflection and inner growth, a time of overcoming strife and contention. There he married into Midianite aristocracy.

4. Near Mount Horeb Jehovah appeared to Moses in the bush that burned but was not consumed. "Horeb" means "solitude," and the burning bush symbolizes the "still small voice" of intuition and wisdom that burns within, which is heard in solitude. To follow its promptings leads one into greater prosperity than ever before.

5. Jehovah informed Moses he was to deliver the enslaved Israelites from Egyptian bondage. Once Moses was assured that Jehovah would help him perform this gigantic task, he set out on his mission promptly.

6. One of the missions of Moses was to show the Children of Israel they had a divine nature within them, called the *"I AM,"* which would lead them out of bondage. The name of the universal God-power which would help them was *"I AM THAT I AM."*

7. The *third* period of Moses' life was spent in the wilderness, molding the unruly Hebrew slaves into a self-sufficient and prosperous nation.

8. He had learned the inner laws of prosperity well, as shown in the way he provided food and water for such a large company in that barren place. There he erected the lavish portable tabernacle in which the Hebrews worshipped.

9. This last forty-year period of Moses' life was a time of ups and downs for the Hebrews, a period of stabilization and inner growth for them.

10. The mission of Moses was a prosperity mission as he helped the Hebrews realize that God was the source of their supply—not the Egyptians. Through use of the inner laws of prosperity, Moses led the Hebrews out of Egyptian bondage, provided for them through their wilderness wanderings, and led them to the edge of their Promised Land of wealth and lavish abundance.

THE PROSPERITY LAW OF CAUSE AND EFFECT

— Chapter 2 —

Before considering the specific prosperity methods that Moses used, let us review the basic success law that he emphasized. The basic law of success is that of cause and effect. Moses has been described as "the great Law Giver" because he constantly pointed out this basic prosperity law to his followers.

According to the law of cause and effect, you are always successful, because you are always getting results from what you think and say!

The law of cause and effect states that as you sow, so shall you also reap. As you give, so shall you receive. Every effect in your life began with a mental cause. When you choose your thoughts, you choose results. What you think, that you become.

WHY SHE HAD EYE TROUBLE

We see the law of cause and effect at work all the time—either in a positive or negative way.

33

There once was a lady who was suffering with her eyes. Her inner wisdom was filled with negative thoughts. She constantly dwelled upon what was wrong with people and situations, instead of looking for what was right. Her body reflected her negative attitudes by manifesting bad health, instead of good.

She attended a church that believed in spiritual healing. She often whined to her church friends, "Why aren't my eyes healed?" In the next breath she would complain, "It was too hot (or too cold) in church today." Or "It was too crowded in church today." Or "Where was everybody?" As she constantly dwelled upon what she thought was wrong with others, she constantly reflected some type of wrong in her own life.

One day a friend of hers said, "I have tried so hard to help Mary get a healing of her eyes. But she refuses to change her attitudes. She refuses to see anything good in life or people. She insists upon seeing all that is wrong."

The friend continued, "The last time I went to see her, Mary even accused me of a lot of negative things I knew nothing about."

This unhappy woman proved that when you "run down" other people, you open the way for some phase of your own life to become "run down." She was a complete success— in her use of the law of cause and effect—but in a negative sense.

HOW ANOTHER'S EYES WERE HEALED

Another lady had a complete healing of her eyes after she began deliberately fasting from negative thinking. She realized she must let go of criticism of herself and others in order to let go of ill health. Her method was this: For an entire year she spent periods daily forgiving and releasing all those people who had previously condemned and criticized her. She said it took her an entire year to be able to hold better thoughts about some of them. But it was worth it. Within that year, her vision was completely healed. An added bonus was that during that period, she also received a large gift of money from one of the people she had just spent a year forgiving!

MEET THE PROSPEROUS MYSTIC

Moses was one of the greatest men who ever lived because he was the first among the ancient leaders to point out publicly the prosperity law of cause and effect. This is the basic law for all true success. Moses pointed out this basic success secret in his famous Ten Commandments, and in the various inner and outer laws that he laid down to help mold the unruly Hebrews slaves from Egypt into a prosperous, self-sufficient, free nation.

Given such titles as "the Initiate," "the first Sage," "the Prince of the Law," the multi-talented Moses was all these and more. He was a practical mystic, a prosperous mystic. A mystic is one who lives from within outwardly as he uses the inner laws of the mind to meet his practical needs in the outer world. Moses did this very successfully. He taught thousands of his followers how to do this so well that the prosperity consciousness they developed is available to you, too, as you faithfully apply their methods.

Moses' life is a tremendous study in the power of thought. In the life of Moses, there is found more about the working of the mind than in all the writings of modern psychology. Why?

Because the ancient Egyptian world, in which Moses was reared, knew and taught the inner laws of the mind and how to invoke them through the power of thought. (Acts 7:22) It was a secret teaching usually given only to the priests and the elect, such as the Royal Family, of which Moses was a part. As a prince at the court of Pharaoh, Moses was instructed in mind power and how to use it. The secret of mind power was considered too powerful to be shared with the enslaved masses, who would only have used it to free themselves from King Pharaoh's cruel bondage.

Moses has been described as "the grand man of the Old Testament" because he did just that: He led the enslaved Hebrews out of cruel Egyptian bondage and a "hard-work consciousness" which they had endured for centuries.

The story of Moses begins in the Book of Exodus. This is significant because the word "exodus" means "to make an exit, to go out." The Book of Exodus shows you how to get out of bondage to financial limitation and to hardships of every kind.

Moses got the Hebrews out of bondage through the deliberate, constructive use of certain mental laws. The events in the life of Moses and his followers symbolize the states of mind and the use of mental laws which you and I can use to be led out of bondage into greater freedom than we have ever known—freedom from ill health, financial problems, family conflicts, spiritual confusion.

NOTHING NEW ABOUT THIS PROSPERITY SYMBOLOGY

There is nothing new about the prosperity symbology in which the Bible is cloaked. Mystical minds have always searched out the success and prosperity symbology of the Bible, which is given in allegory and in symbols.[1]

It was a common method used by spiritual teachers throughout history—both Catholic and Protestant—including Bernard of Clairvaux, St. John of the Cross, Jeremy Taylor, and John Wesley. As early as 180 A.D., Pentaenus, Clement, and Origen taught this success symbology based upon metaphysical Bible interpretation in the excellent Christian University at Alexandria.

They derived the metaphysical meaning of the Bible teachings by tracing significant Bible words and names back to their root meaning, based on the original Hebrew, Greek, and Aramaic words, from which they were originally translated. The prosperity secrets of Moses become obvious as we do the same thing in this book.

Metaphysical interpretation has been secretly taught by occult groups down through the ages, but it has not been generally taught to the masses. The great people of the Bible were master psychologists and metaphysicians who strove constantly to teach the power of mental attitudes for success or failure.

In this enlightened age into which we enter, the prosperity symbology of the Bible is going to come into its own!

---

1. Unless otherwise indicated, the Biblical passages quoted in this book are from the American Standard Version of the Holy Bible.

The time is ripe to teach the masses, instead of just a select few, how the power of thought can produce either abundance or financial limitation in their lives.

NO ONE CAN WITHHOLD YOUR GOOD

You can stop blaming other people for your problems. Because of the success law of cause and effect, no one can take your good from you. No one can keep your good from you but yourself. When you choose your thoughts, you choose results. When you change your thoughts, you change results.

For this purpose remind yourself often: *"No person, thing or event can keep from me that which the universe has for me now. I claim my unlimited good now. I call the wealth of the universe into expression for me here and now."*

So many people erroneously think their good is dependent upon someone else. They say, "I wish my husband (or wife) would think this way. *Then* we could prosper."

You are master of your fate. *When you change, your world changes.* It is up to you. Your good is not dependent upon other people, situations, or conditions. Your good is dependent only upon your good thinking about it. No one can give greater good to you until you have first opened your mind to receive it.

A marvelous statement to help open our minds to receive is this: *"No one can delay my good. No one can withhold my good. I am open and receptive to my highest good in mind, body, and financial affairs here and now."*

You need only announce the good and stand by it. It is the good thought that starts your good into action!

HOW GOOD THINGS HAPPENED TO THE AUTHOR

During one period in my life, it seemed that other people were keeping my good from me. To help change my thinking, I clipped these words from a magazine and placed them where I could see them every day as I went about my work: *"Good things begin to happen now."* That method worked. When I no longer gave power to outside situations, my good began coming to me both in seen and in unforeseen ways.

Stop trying to change people and conditions outwardly. Stop tampering with the outer picture. Stop trying to fix things up. Stop trying to force your good to you. Stop trying to make over other people.

Instead, start changing and improving yourself. Do so by announcing the good: *"Wherever I am, good things happen."* Then stand by it. Start changing your own thinking, improving it, and uplifting it. As you do, your life will improve. This is the success law of cause and effect. What you think, that you become.

GAIN CONTROL OF YOUR WORLD THROUGH WORDS

When in the throes of unhappy experiences, you may not be able to reverse your thoughts right away, but you can reverse your *words*. Repetition of right words impresses both the conscious and subconscious phases of your world through your words. *You can transform your life by transforming your thinking about your life through your words.*

HOW HE WENT FROM $6,500 TO A $30,000 INCOME

A prominent Protestant minister proved this. He had a
large congregation. He was well-known and highly re-
spected. Yet his church was paying him only $6,500 a year.
Naturally he resented this small income which was inade-
quate to meet the needs of his growing family. His was a
prosperous church which could have easily paid far more,
but those in charge had the old erroneous idea that a minister was supposed to be kept poor in order to keep him
"humble." Instead of keeping him "humble," a limited income only kept this minister resentful and in debt.

As pointed out later in this book, the priests of the Old
Testament became millionaires through the tithing laws
set down by Moses. *Being a practical mystic, Moses knew
that those in spiritual work needed to be freed from financial strain in order to devote their time and energies
fully to their own spiritual growth and to the spiritual welfare of their followers.*

This Protestant minister came upon my book, *The Dynamic Laws of Prosperity,* which pointed out that *all* people were the rich children of a loving Father; that this was
their spiritual heritage. This man realized that this heritage
even included ministers, and he decided to do something
about it!

He began to change his thinking by saying to himself:
*"Regardless of the kind of work I do, I can still be pros-
perous. I should be prosperous. It is my divine heritage to
be prosperous. Therefore, I claim my heritage of unlimited
prosperity now."*

His expanded thinking quickly expanded his world. He was soon asked by his denomination to take over a regional job for them. He did so, thinking it meant giving his services free of charge while continuing with his church work. Instead he was paid $30,000 the next year for this special assignment. As he continued gaining control of his world through his daily use of prosperous words, he went on to other spiritual work that offered far greater freedom and financial compensation that he had ever known before. His financial income has continued to soar.

When you deliberately change your world by changing your words about it, everything begins to come your way. This is how the prosperity law of cause and effect works in a constructive way.

ONE OF MOSES' GREATEST PROSPERITY SECRETS

The word "Moses" means "to draw out." One of Moses' greatest prosperity secrets was that he knew how to draw the good out of apparently negative experiences. When you too learn how to do that, your prosperity is just around the corner! You've "got it made."

Shortly after his birth, Moses' mother placed him in an ark in the bulrushes. It was there that Pharaoh's daughter found him, and asked her servant to draw him out of the water. The water out of which Moses was drawn symbolizes the negative side of life, which always contains possibilities for good.

You can draw the good out of disappointing experiences as you dwell on this basic prosperity principle: *"Nothing*

*is evil that brings forth good. There is good in every ex-
perience, and I draw it forth now."*

HOW A MARRIAGE WAS RESTORED AFTER
ELEVEN YEARS' SEPARATION

A career woman in Pennsylvania recently wrote:

"I was on a treadmill of nervousness and dissatisfaction
when I first learned that there is good in every experience.
This was a new idea to me. I still worked every day at
a good paying job, but I just went to work, came home,
cooked, cleaned, and took care of my child. I never went
out. Just work and sleep, usually with a few drinks be-
for retiring. I didn't care how I looked and I had the
sloppy appearance to prove it. I was a real dull person
of 33.

"Then I began to dwell on the thought, *'There is good
for me, I ought to have it, and I draw it forth now.'* I
had read these inspirational words somewhere. Little by
little things started happening. To let go of the past and
to believe I could improve my life began to catch on.

"Almost overnight a new world opened to me as I hung
on to that thought. I had certain goals, but obstacles
(mostly my own negative thinking) kept getting in the
way.

"How did I draw forth good out of my negative thinking and dull life? First, I began talking to God every
day about my life and about the things I wished to accomplish. I also wrote a letter to God every day asking
His help. I began to think of myself as a spiritual being
living in a good world. I even pronounced my dull, dull
life 'good.' *That* took faith.

"Things started to move, changing and improving as I brought the thought of God's good more and more into my daily thoughts and feelings. On the weekend of April 13th, which was two months after I started trying this method, everything broke loose:

"I had a husband whom I had never divorced although we had been separated for eleven years. I went to see him to discuss something about our son. We occasionally did this. On this visit, one thing led to another and we finally talked to each other and listened to each other for the first time in eleven years. We even discussed whether we could still make a go of our marriage. Frankly we didn't know whether it was even possible.

"When I returned home from that trip, I sat down and quietly wrote out the problems involved, asking God for His guidance. Was another try at our marriage His good for us? My son thought so. He was elated over the possibilities of living with both his parents. The next day I met a friend who was interested in disposing of our house in case I went back to live with my husband in his home. On Tuesday I quietly investigated all the facts concerning a possible transfer with my company to the town where my husband lived. By the end of the week, all major problems were on the way to being resolved. The following weekend my husband paid us a visit. Together we worked out a budget and discovered that financially, we could make it much easier together than apart.

"We are now back together and a whole new life has opened to all three of us. I know I have experienced a miracle. *When you contact God's good by dwelling upon it, you can change years of problems overnight! Yes, nothing is evil that brings forth good.*"

THE PATH TO PERMANENTLY INCREASING
PROSPERITY

The drawing forth of good out of unhappy experiences always works from within out. It is when you are weak as water from negative experiences that, like Moses, you are ready for great growth, which always leads to great good. I have seen it happen over and over again in my own life, as well as in the lives of others.

One last observation: Moses was the youngest son of Amram and Jochebed. The word "Amram" means "exalted people." The word "Jochebed" means "honorable and great." When you use the success law of cause and effect, as described in this chapter, to dwell upon the positive and good in life, you too become exalted in your thinking. This paves the way for a great and honorable life to open to you!

As you proceed with the prosperity methods set forth by Moses in the pages of this book, I trust that you too shall draw forth great good from all of your experiences. As you do so, you shall surely be on the path to permanently increasing prosperity, even to unlimited wealth!

A MEDITATION TO HELP YOU USE
THE PROSPERITY LAW OF CAUSE AND EFFECT

For this purpose, you will enjoy declaring often, "ACCORD-
ING TO THE LAW OF CAUSE AND EFFECT, I AM ALWAYS
SUCCESSFUL, BECAUSE I AM ALWAYS GETTING RESULTS FROM
WHAT I THINK AND SAY. THE LAW OF CAUSE AND EFFECT
STATES THAT AS I SOW, SO SHALL I ALSO REAP. AS I GIVE, SO
SHALL I RECEIVE. EVERY EFFECT IN MY LIFE BEGAN WITH A
MENTAL CAUSE. WHEN I CHOOSE MY THOUGHTS, I CHOOSE
RESULTS. WHAT I THINK, THAT I BECOME.

"I CAN TRANSFORM MY LIFE BY TRANSFORMING MY WORDS
ABOUT MY LIFE. NO ONE CAN DELAY MY GOOD. NO ONE CAN
WITHHOLD MY GOOD. I AM OPEN AND RECEPTIVE TO MY HIGH-
EST GOOD, SO GOOD THINGS BEGIN TO HAPPEN NOW! YES,
WHEN I DELIBERATELY CHANGE MY WORLD BY CHANGING MY
WORDS ABOUT IT, EVERYTHING BEGINS TO COME MY WAY.

"THERE IS GOOD FOR ME, I OUGHT TO HAVE IT, AND I DRAW
IT FORTH NOW. NOTHING IS EVIL THAT BRINGS FORTH GOOD.
WHEN I CONTACT GOD'S GOOD BY DWELLING UPON IT, I CAN
CHANGE YEARS OF PROBLEMS OVERNIGHT!

"REGARDLESS OF THE KIND OF WORK I DO—OR THE CIR-
CUMSTANCES OF MY LIFE—I CAN STILL BE PROSPEROUS. I
SHOULD BE PROSPEROUS. IT IS MY DIVINE HERITAGE TO
PROSPER. THEREFORE, I CLAIM MY HERITAGE OF UNLIMITED
PROSPERITY NOW."

SUMMARY

1. The basic law of prosperity is that of cause and effect. Moses has been described as "the great Law Giver" because he constantly pointed out this basic prosperity law to his followers.

2. According to the law of cause and effect, you are always successful, because you are always getting results from what you think and say: As you sow, so shall you also reap. As you give, so shall you receive.

3. When you choose your thoughts, you choose results. What you think and say, that you become. Moses pointed this out in the Ten Commandments and throughout his teachings.

4. A mystic is one who lives from within outwardly as he uses the inner laws of the mind to meet his practical needs in the outer world. Moses was a "practical mystic" because he did this very successfully and taught thousands of his followers how to do so, too.

5. Moses had learned about the power of thought and how to use it to prosper one's self and others while a member of the Royal Family at the court of Pharaoh in Egypt.

6. The story of Moses begins in the Book of Exodus. The word "exodus" means "to make an exit." The Book of Exodus relates Moses' experiences showing how to get out of bondage to financial limitation and limitation of every kind.

7. There is nothing new about the prosperity symbology in which the Bible is cloaked. It was commonly known by great spiritual teachers throughout history as they traced significant Bible words and names back to their root meaning based on the original Hebrew, Greek, and Aramaic meaning.

8. Because of the success law of cause and effect, no one can take your good from you. No one can keep your good from you except yourself. When you change your thoughts, you change results. When you change, your world changes.

9. You can transform your life by transforming your thinking about your life through your words. When you deliberately change your world by changing your words about it, everything begins to come your way.

10. The word "Moses" means "to draw out." One of Moses' greatest prosperity secrets was that he learned how to draw the good out of apparently negative experiences. When you too learn how to do this, your prosperity is assured.

THE PROSPERITY LAW
OF FEARLESSNESS

— Chapter 3 —

Through use of the prosperity law of fearlessness, you can get out of Egyptian bondage symbolizing financial limitation, and you can cross your Red Seas, which symbolize all kinds of difficulties.

Almost everyone in the world today is in bondage to something. We are in the process of overcoming limited thinking and restricted living in some form. But this is for a purpose. It is through our bondage experiences that we "come to ourselves" inwardly and outwardly. Your bondage experiences motivate you to want to rise out of limitation and to go forward to something better!

The great cause of bondage is this:

Most of us have believed that we were helped or hurt by other people, that we received our good from outside circumstances, people, or events. But our good really comes to us from *within* our own being. God in us is the fountainhead of all our good. When you realize this, nothing that anyone does or says, or fails to do or say, can shake you up or keep you from claiming your good.

For this purpose, you will enjoy declaring these words:

"My good cannot be withheld from me. My good cannot be taken from me. No person, thing or event can keep that from me which the universe has for me now. The universe has unlimited good for me, and I accept it, receive it, and experience it now."

When I learned this prosperity secret, it was the turning point in my life, from lifelong poverty to one of a gradually increasing affluence. I could almost feel the shackles of poverty falling away when I began boldly to declare often the foregoing words.

This is what Moses tried to show the Hebrews. They considered themselves slaves in Egypt. Moses pointed out that they need not remain slaves to the Egyptians. As children of God, they were heirs to all good. Jehovah assured them their own Promised Land flowing with milk and honey. But they had to rise out of the financial limitation imposed by the ruthless Egyptians first. *They had to make the effort to claim their Promised Land of abundance, and so must you!*

It is time to awaken to the great Truth that you are not a servant to life's difficulties. No, you are an heir to the unlimited good of the universe! This lavish good only awaits your recognition and acceptance of it. The success law of fearlessness shows you how to claim it.

You can begin by declaring: *"I am a child of the universe. I am a child of fortune. So I claim my universal wealth. I claim my good fortune now."*

HOW TO GET OUT OF BONDAGE

At the time Moses appeared on the scene, the Hebrews were in great trouble. They did not know how to get out of bondage. *A loving Father always sends a Moses to help us get out of our bondage experiences, too.* Here Moses symbolizes the laws of mind action. He shows us how to use our mind powers constructively so that we are freed from the troublesome experiences of life. (The universal success laws pointed out in this book are our "Moses.")

The first way to get out of bondage to life's difficulties is to make the effort. Even though he was a giant in the use of mind-power, Moses had to persist in claiming freedom from Pharaoh, and so must you. Pharaoh symbolizes any problem from which you want freedom. Moses appeared before Pharaoh again and again saying, "Let my people go." (Exodus 5:1; 7:16; 8:1, 20; 9:1, 13; 10:3)

You will never get out of bondage until you begin to speak words of freedom, rather than talking about the problem. When you talk and talk about your problems, you bind them to you because the description of evil multiplies evil. The Hebrews had repeatedly cried out against their taskmasters rather than speaking words of freedom from them.

An important step in getting out of bondage is to stop talking about it. Negative situations want you to feel bad about them. Your disturbed words feed negation and keep it alive in your life. When you stop feeling bad about negative appearances, they fade away for lack of attention. When you release them, you become freed from them.

To the pharaohs of bondage in your life, speak these

words of freedom: *"It is not so. My life cannot be limited. My good cannot be limited. I claim my freedom. I claim my unlimited good now."*

HOW MARRIAGE CAME TO A WIDOW

At the beginning of a Lenten season, a widow of ten years began to say: *"My life cannot be limited. Christ in me now frees me from all limitation. My life now becomes far happier than it has ever been before. I rejoice in my newfound happiness now!"*

During that Lenten season, she met a fine widower at church. He invited her to lunch, then to dinner. She thought, "This man is like a member of the family. He is so comfortable to be with." They had a June wedding and have been busy "living happily ever after" ever since.

THE PROSPERITY POWER OF PERSISTENCE

When Jehovah told Moses he was to go to Pharaoh and demand freedom for the Hebrews, Moses objected because he was not a good speaker. Jehovah sent Moses' brother, Aaron, along to help him.

The word "Aaron" symbolizes strength. It took great strength for Moses to appear repeatedly before Pharaoh and ask for freedom, especially when his requests were not being granted. By having to appear before Pharaoh a number of times and speak words of freedom, Moses gained an inner strength which he would need later—not only to get the Hebrews out of bondage, but to keep them out of it.

When you try to overcome a problem and do not succeed, you have not failed. You are merely gaining an inner strength through your repeated efforts, which you will need to make your demonstration and to keep it. Like Moses, "If at first you don't succeed, try, try again."

(If the Hebrews had been released by Pharaoh immediately upon their first request for freedom, they would not have survived their wilderness experiences because they would not have gained the understanding and inner strength needed to do so.)

Speak the word of freedom when you are trying to overcome a problem: *"The power of God is working through me to free me from every negative influence. Nothing can hold me in bondage. No one can oppose my good. I am an overcomer, a child of God, so I now accomplish great things with ease."* If that freedom does not come immediately, you have taken a step toward your desired goal. When you have taken enough steps toward your goal, you will step right into it. Then you will need all the inner strength you have developed to assist you in maintaining that new good.

HOW THE SUCCESS POWER OF PERSISTENCE
WORKED FOR THE AUTHOR

It is often when you have struggled until you feel you cannot go on that your good begins to appear. Meanwhile your struggles were not wasted. The work was being done in the invisible.

It is through persistently claiming your freedom, even in the face of apparent failure, that you come through defeat undefeated. *Persistence is a first requirement for getting out of bondage.* Moses proved it, and so can you!

It once took me ten years to get free of bondage to a certain problem. For long periods I felt I could not go on trying; the bondage seemed endless. Yet something in me made me go on. I had nothing to go back to.

When freedom finally came, I realized that every effort in that direction had been getting me ready for the final overcoming. Had it not been for the continuous effort, I would not have gained the inner strength needed to make the demonstration, nor the insight to keep it.

HOW THE PLAGUES WERE BLESSINGS IN DISGUISE

The Hebrews had gone to Egypt to live in order to escape a famine during the era when their famous kinsman, Joseph, was Prime Minister. The Egyptians did not object to having the Hebrews there as long as Joseph lived. He had been their saviour from starvation. But after his death the Egyptians resented the Hebrews. They felt the Hebrews were mercenary and were taking food right out of their very mouths. There were even race riots in Egypt in 1300 B.C.

In order to placate the Egyptians, the Hebrews became common laborers. They were allowed to receive three meals a day and to live in the slum areas, as long as they worked as slave labor. Pharaoh ordered all male Hebrew children killed, hoping their population would die out. Moses then appeared on the scene to free them from all this misery.

But they were not yet willing to be freed, or to leave the scene of their misery.

Often we have been like the Hebrews, who did not appreciate Moses when he tried to rescue them. We do not always recognize or welcome the guidance that comes to us which is trying to free us from bondage. *When you have gotten the good out of an old situation, it becomes bondage to you. It no longer satisfies you and you may complain about it. Yet you usually are not willing to make the effort to gain freedom from that bondage.*

HOW TO HANDLE IT WHEN THINGS GET WORSE

There were ten plagues connected with Moses' pleas for freedom for his people. Those plagues seemed cruel but they actually were blessings in disguise. They would not have been necessary had the Hebrews been willing to leave Egypt on their own, but they were not. They reasoned that it was safer to endure slavery in Egypt than to face the unknown on their own. It took those harassing plagues to force the Hebrews to let go and get out of an old situation which they had outgrown—to get out at any cost. They had bound themselves to something that had run its course in their growth, something from which they needed freedom.

When you want freedom from bondage, you must first be willing to let that bondage go. As long as you are willing to continue living with that limitation, you will have to simply because you have not released it. But when an experience has run its course in your life, and you still continue to bow down to it, that limitation "hardens its heart" toward you, and things get worse in order to force you to let go.

Things may get all stirred up when you begin to speak words of freedom. *But your plagues are an indication that freedom is on the way.* Instead of being frightened by such periods of chemicalization, this is the time to rejoice by declaring: *"I rejoice and give thanks because freedom is on the way!"* Then let go again and again and again, if necessary to make way for your new good. (See the chapter on Chemicalization in my book, *The Dynamic Laws of Healing.*)

Up until the ninth plague, Pharaoh tried to compromise with Moses. He said he would allow the Children of Israel to go out into the wilderness and sacrifice to their God, but they must return to Egypt. Moses refused to compromise. Through nine plagues he said, "No." The number "nine" symbolizes the finishing of an old cycle and the beginning of a new one.

When you speak words of freedom to a problem, you will be tested. Always there will be the possibility of compromise. *If you accept that compromise, you will remain in bondage.* Like Moses, you may have to say "no" many times. When you refuse to settle for a compromise, then your complete freedom comes.

With the tenth and last plague, Pharaoh not only released the Hebrews, he wanted them to leave. In the tenth plague, one of his own children died. At this point the Hebrews could not have stopped their freedom. They could not have stayed in Egypt, even if they had wanted to. They were literally pushed out of bondage by the very force that had previously bound them! The thing from which they wanted freedom suddenly wanted freedom from them.

Even though the Hebrews were suddenly under great pressure to leave Egypt, they did not do so until they first did something very significant: They observed the Passover which was an ancient festival associated with the offering of a portion of the flocks and crops— a prosperity festival. It was an observance in recognition of God's help and blessings a celebration of answered prayer for having "passed over" so much.

With thanksgiving that their prayers for release from bondage had been answered and that freedom was on the way, they quietly feasted. They offered gifts of their finest cattle as sacrifices and thank offerings in appreciation of answered prayer. Even though they needed to leave quickly, they did not do so until they had put God first, asking His divine guidance and protection. Throughout their history, when the Hebrews remembered to do this, all their needs were met. (Chapter 8 describes the prospering power of thanksgiving.)

Then they left quickly and uneventfully amid the darkness, yet they left rejoicing. They knew that the number "ten" was the number of light, as well as the number of increased good (tenth plague).

You often get your freedom from bondage when things are darkest in your life. The mystics knew that after "the dark night of the soul" comes answered prayer. *It is darkest just before the dawn of new good.*

THE PROSPERING POWER OF
LETTING GO GRACIOUSLY

When your freedom comes, it can come so quickly that
it is breathtaking. *Accept it on its own terms quickly and
nonresistantly, whether it comes in the way you had in mind
or not.* You are past the "point of no return."

There once was a man who wanted freedom from a job he
had had for twenty years, but he felt helpless to do anything
about it. His employer had assured him he had the best
job in town in his category.

His wife started picturing a better job for her husband
anyway. She began to speak words of freedom: *"There are
better things ahead for us."* Soon this man received word
that he had been thoroughly investigated for a fine government job. This position offered increased pay, benefits
from a retirement program, sick leave, and other financial
blessings that his present job did not offer.

When he appeared for an interview he was quickly hired.
At first he was glad. Then he began to feel badly about leav-
ing his friends and the familiar surroundings of his old job.
He continued to feel distressed until his employer said
bluntly, "When you leave, do not come back for any reason. You are finished here, so do not tarry." It was a surprise, a shock, to hear these words. But they freed him to
go to his new good quickly with no regrets.

HOW HE LOST A JOB BUT GAINED A POSITION

Another man held a job for fifteen years—a job he had hated. He felt it was his financial security so he put up with a lot just to hold on to it. Yet all the time, he was mentally trying to get his freedom from it. One day that freedom came when a change in organization eliminated his job. He was stunned as he thought, "How could they do this to me? I gave them fifteen years of faithful service."

In his humiliation, he talked with a friend who reminded him that he had wanted freedom from this job. Perhaps it had seemed a surprise when suddenly the job he had wanted freedom from, wanted freedom from him! Nevertheless, the friend convinced him he had lost nothing; he had everything to gain because he had been freed from what he did not want. He was now free to claim what he did want.

Soon he had the finest job of his life. At last he was at peace. This man had lost a job but he had gained a position. When he accepted freedom from bondage on its own terms, it opened the way to a new life. He was no longer making a living. He was making a life. He proved that *it pays to accept your freedom graciously, regardless of how it comes.*

WHAT TO DO WHEN BONDAGE TRIES TO RECAPTURE YOU

Although the Hebrews left Egypt rejoicing, soon they were in doubting states of mind again. The Egyptians had followed them. When they realized this, they forgot all about the freedom Moses had just obtained for them. Instead they severely criticized him saying, "Would it not have been better that we serve the Egyptians than that we die in the wilderness?" (Exodus 14:12)

Have you ever gained freedom from a problem, only to have it flare up again? So you doubted, criticized, condemned?

After you get out of bondage, you may be tested. Just as the Egyptians tried to overtake the Hebrews, so an old condition may often try to overtake you again. If it does, realize what is happening. Then keep your thinking straight and do the fearless thing. This will strengthen your new good and make you secure in it. You can do this by declaring: *"I am fearless and free in God's love for me. I claim my complete freedom now and I keep it."*

A person beset by difficulties will often apply himself mentally in zealously solving his problems. That is just the beginning. If he gets mentally lax afterwards, his good does not last. So a time of testing can be for good. It keeps him from getting careless.

WHY HER DEMONSTRATION FADED

There once was a lady who wanted to get married. She worked mentally to attract a husband and did so. After her marriage she stopped thinking positively. She stopped attending success classes and church services where she had learned how to use mind power constructively to improve her life. She dropped out of sight, confident in her new good.

Months later she appeared again greatly shaken. The man she had married had "changed his mind" about their marriage and quietly left town. Her demonstration had faded.

HOW TO KEEP YOUR GOOD BY HOLDING YOUR PEACE

When the Hebrews saw the Egyptians following them, they became very critical of Moses, but he would have none of their criticism:

> "Fear not, stand still. See the salvation of the Lord, which He will work for you this day. The Egyptians whom ye have seen this day, ye shall see no more forever. Jehovah will fight for you, and you shall hold your peace."
>
> (Exodus 14:13, 14)

Here is your success formula when old conditions try to flare up again:

1. "Fear not, stand still." Get quiet and stay quiet about the problem.
2. "See the salvation of the Lord." In your quietness, believe in and declare complete deliverance: "God is *my defense and my deliverance now.*" Then expect it.

If you dare to stand firm at this point by quietly believing in and accepting your new good only, the former problems that tried to flare up will suddenly be gone forever. *But you must hold your peace to bring it about.*

Old problems that have lost their grip on us die hard. But fade away they will if we refuse to get upset and excited when they try to reappear in our lives. Say: *"No, I do not accept this as lasting or real in my life. This is not so. It is now gone forever."* Hold to that thought and it will become so.

HOW HE AVOIDED A LAWSUIT BY KEEPING QUIET

While driving on a rainy day, a traveling salesman was in an accident. He was stopped when a truck suddenly jack-knifed in front of him, causing him to be hit by a car from behind.

Although his car was totally demolished, he miraculously walked away from the accident scene, shaken but unharmed. His insurance company felt he should not sue. They insisted that, legally, all involved were equally responsible. His attorney felt he could collect heavily if he did sue both other parties.

Being a student of the power of thought, this man felt he did not want to expend himself mentally or emotionally trying to collect money through a lawsuit. He reasoned that the time spent and the negative vibrations set up would cost him far more than he could collect. He dismissed the matter. He also kept his accident experience quiet and discussed it with no one but his insurance company and his attorney.

Months later, it tried to flare up again. He learned that

both other drivers were planning to sue him, although he had been the only party who had suffered damages. Instead of getting upset over the injustice of it all, this man "stood still." He mentioned the possibilities of lawsuits to no one. He insisted upon complete deliverance from all negative possibilities by declaring daily: *"I do not accept this. It is not so. God is my defense and my complete deliverance from this situation now and forever. It is done, finished, completed now. The subject is closed."*

Soon both parties "changed their minds" and dropped their lawsuits against him. He never heard from them again. In his happiness over these events, he went forth and made new business contacts which more than compensated him financially for the losses he had suffered.

Chiropractic treatments not only straightened out his unnerving reactions to the accident, but a health problem of long standing was discovered and corrected in the process. Had it not been, it could have caused him undue suffering and financial expense later. Thus his accident experience had been a blessing in disguise, but only after he held his peace about it.

HOW TO CROSS YOUR RED SEA

When the Hebrews got to the Red Sea, Moses lifted up his rod and stretched forth his hand over the sea. He knew it would divide as his followers did the fearless thing and walked into the sea upon his instruction. They passed through the sea effortlessly on dry land. The waters, which had parted before them, then united behind them. The Egyptians pursuing them were all drowned.

When challenges confront you, don't try to avoid them. Instead of getting excited about them, get very quiet. Do the fearless thing: Stretch forth some idea of good over the uncertain situation. Speak your words of good until you feel that good stretching out over the entire situation, covering it like a cloak. The challenge will then divide and begin to open up to you. You will pass through it, divinely protected, to your new good.

Nothing happened—the Red Sea did not part—until the Hebrews did something fearless. They were not allowed merely to look at it from a distance and hopefully wait for it to part, thinking that when it did, *then* they would go through it to dry land. At Moses' command they went forward right into the Sea. They had to walk up to it and do the fearless thing.

HOW A DYING WOMAN RECOVERED

You can always cross your Red Seas unharmed by doing the fearless thing. When you walk up to it, lift up your thinking about it, stretch forth some idea of good over it, then your challenge will begin to part, diminish, and fade away.

Sometimes the most fearless thing you can do is to speak good words in the face of opposing appearances.

I once visited a lady who had been hospitalized for many weeks. She was not expected to live. When I prayerfully spoke words of healing for her with my eyes closed, I had the feeling she never even bothered to close her eyes. Yet that was the turning point. She recovered. When good words were fearlessly spoken for her, she did go forward to new wholeness, though everyone involved had expected her to die.

HOW $400 CAME TO A HOUSEWIFE

Perhaps you are trying to cross a Red Sea of financial difficulties. If so, do something fearless. Face the financial challenge by saying to it, "You do not scare me." Then stretch forth your thinking over the situation by declaring: *"Divine Substance cannot be withheld from me now. Divine Substance is the one and only reality in this situation. Divine Substance is available, and Divine Substance is doing its bountiful work here and now. Knowing this, I have faith that every need is now met."*

In some way Divine Substance will come to your rescue. If you do not do the fearless thing at this point, you will just stand looking at your Red Sea of difficulties indefinitely and fearfully. This holds those difficulties in your life.

A housewife had several hundred dollars' worth of bills due. She waited for money to appear with which to pay them. Nothing happened until she realized that she must do something fearless. She had just $10 left in her checking account. She wrote out a check giving this amount to her church. It was a "faith offering" given in the belief that additional money would appear.

She said to a friend, "I am going to demonstrate the prosperity I need because I have just done the fearless thing.

I have given, so I have opened the way to receive." It happened. She soon received $400 for some work she had done months earlier for which she had never been paid.

HOW DOING THE FEARLESS THING BROUGHT
NEW PROSPERITY TO A CHURCH

During a cold winter when church offerings had been low, the treasurer said, "We've got to do something to demonstrate prosperity in order to pay all these bills, but what can we do?"

The thought came, "Do the fearless thing. Give." Boldly he said to the other trustees, "Bills are due and the offerings have been low. We've got to do something to demonstrate increased prosperity. Let's send today's entire offering as a gift to the mother church. Holding on to that amount won't pay many of our bills anyway. We cannot afford *not* to give if we want to demonstrate the increased prosperity we need for our own church right now. Let's do the fearless thing."

Hesitantly the trustees agreed. Their method worked. By the end of the next week, so many tithes and offerings had flowed into the church, that more money had come in during that one week than during the entire previous month! The bills were all paid and there was a surplus.

DOING THE FEARLESS THING WORKED FOR
THE AUTHOR

In my early days in the ministry, I was scheduled to attend an out-of-state ministers' conference. For professional reasons, I needed to do so. But it was a challenge to make the effort, because I had only $10 with which to leave town. The church I was serving was in modest financial circumstances, and I did not feel I should ask them to pay the entire expense of my trip, although it was customarily done.

Instead, as I prayed for guidance and supply, a couple from the church, who were attending, offered to drive me hundreds of miles to the conference. Another couple in attendance offered to pay for my meals. I was given a church check with which to pay for my hotel room at the conclusion of my stay. And I had been invited to do some lecture work in the conference area, which I hoped would pay my plane fare home. (The friends driving me to the conference planned to remain on afterwards in the area to vacation.)

It was an unnerving experience to leave town on such a long trip with only $10 in my pocket. However, no one knew my financial situation so they placed no limitations upon me. As I kept quiet and blessed that $10, my needs were met, and everything worked out fine. I trust I will never find myself in similar circumstances again. But if I did, I would use that same success formula: *Keep quiet and do the fearless thing.* It worked.

HOW A PROFESSOR CROSSED HIS RED SEA AND PROSPERED BY GIVING THANKS

After crossing the Red Sea, the Hebrews did something that many people forget to do when their problems have been solved. They sang praises to God, acknowledging the help He had given them. It was a song of deliverance:

"I will sing unto Jehovah, for He has triumphed gloriously. The Lord is my strength and song and He has become my salvation. This is my God and I will praise Him."

(Exodus 15:1, 2)

A college professor made a success map picturing the increased financial income he desired. As he daily looked at that financial map, the increased income came in the form of a new job. Later he looked at his success map to see what had brought results. On his success map he had placed a picture of a bundle of money. Near this picture he had placed the words, "Where did all the money come from?" Below the pictured money was a prayer of thanksgiving, which he had used daily—long before the money had appeared. His prayer had been the words of the Psalmist: "I will sing unto Jehovah, because He hath dealt bountifully with me." (Psalms 13:6)

HOW TO SEAL YOUR GOOD

There is always a way out of bondage—through the use of praise and thanksgiving. By giving thanks for your safe Red Sea crossing, you seal your good and make it permanent. (Chapter 8 describes the prospering power of thanksgiving.)

Declare often: "I will sing unto Jehovah, for He has

triumphed gloriously. The Lord is my strength and my song. He has become my salvation. This is my God and I will praise Him."

A MEDITATION TO HELP YOU USE THE PROSPERITY LAW OF FEARLESSNESS

"THE FIRST WAY TO GET OUT OF BONDAGE TO LIFE'S DIFFICULTIES IS TO MAKE THE EFFORT. I BEGIN TO SPEAK WORDS OF FREEDOM, RATHER THAN TALKING ABOUT THE PROBLEM. I DECLARE, *'The power of God is working through me to free me from every negative influence. Nothing can hold me in bondage. I am an overcomer, a child of God, so I now accomplish great things with ease.'*

"THINGS MAY GET STIRRED UP WHEN I BEGIN TO SPEAK WORDS OF FREEDOM. BUT SUCH PLAGUES ARE AN INDICATION THAT FREEDOM IS ON THE WAY. SO THIS IS A TIME TO GIVE THANKS: *'I rejoice and give thanks because freedom is on the way.'* FREEDOM FROM BONDAGE MAY COME WHEN THINGS ARE DARKEST IN MY LIFE.

"WHEN FREEDOM APPEARS, IT CAN COME SO QUICKLY THAT IT IS BREATHTAKING. I ACCEPT MY FREEDOM ON ITS OWN TERMS QUICKLY AND NON-RESISTANTLY, WHETHER IT COMES IN THE WAY I HAD IN MIND OR NOT. I ACCEPT MY FREEDOM GRACIOUSLY, REGARDLESS OF HOW IT COMES. ONCE MY FREEDOM COMES, I KEEP QUIET ABOUT OLD PROBLEMS, SO THEY WILL NOT TRY TO RE-APPEAR IN MY LIFE. BY GIVING THANKS, I SEAL MY GOOD AND MAKE IT PERMANENT."

SUMMARY

1. Your bondage experiences motivate you to want to rise out of limitation and go forward to something better.

2. Moses tried to show the Hebrews they did not need to remain slaves in Egypt. As children of God they were heirs to all good. Jehovah had assured them of their own Promised Land flowing with milk and honey. But they had to rise out of financial limitation to the Egyptians first. They had to make the effort to claim their Promised Land of abundance, and so must we.

3. A loving Father always sends a Moses to help us out of our bondage experiences. The first way to get out of bondage to life's difficulties is to make the effort.

4. You will never get out of bondage until you begin to speak words of freedom, rather than talking about the problem. An important step in getting free of bondage is to stop talking about it.

5. When Moses appeared before King Pharaoh, Jehovah sent Moses' brother, Aaron, along to help him. The word "Aaron" means "strength." By having to appear before Pharaoh a number of times and speak words of freedom, Moses gained an inner strength which he would need later, not only to get the Hebrews out of bondage, but to keep them out of it.

6. When you try to overcome a problem and do not succeed, you have not failed. You are merely gaining an inner strength through your repeated efforts, which you will need to make your demonstration and to keep it.

7. It is often when you have struggled until you feel you cannot go on that your good begins to appear. Persistence is a first requirement for getting out of bondage.

8. When you want freedom from bondage, you've got to first be willing to let that bondage go. Your plagues are an indication that freedom is on the way. You often get your freedom from bondage when things are darkest in your life. It pays to accept your freedom graciously, regardless of how it comes by observing a "pass over" of thanksgiving.

9. After you get out of bondage, you may be tested. Just as the Egyptians had tried to follow the Hebrews out of Egypt and overtake them, so an old condition may try to overtake you. If it does, keep your thinking straight and do the fearless thing. Then hold your peace. As you do so, the old conditions will fade away completely.

10. You can always cross your Red Seas unharmed by doing the fearless thing. When you do the fearless thing under divine guidance, you always get results. After victoriously crossing the Red Sea, the Hebrews did something that many people forget to do after their problems have been solved: They sang praises to God, acknowledging the help He had given them. By giving thanks for your safe Red Sea crossing, you seal your good, give it protection, and make it permanent.

HOW TO GATHER YOUR PROSPEROUS MANNA

— Chapter 4 —

The word "manna" means "any needed sustenance that seems miraculously supplied."

Any time you have a challenge, especially in a financial form, you need to know how to meet that need by gathering your manna. When you learn how to gather that manna, your need is often supplied in as miraculous a way as were the needs of the Hebrews during their wilderness sojourn.

"Manna" is that substance that comes to us out of the heavenly realms of the mind. We gather it and "eat" it basically through prosperity decrees. *One of the quickest ways to gather your manna is by calling on Divine Substance through repeated prosperity decrees spoken aloud.* This stirs up the wealth of the universe and causes it to be manifested for you in appropriate form. Many people have gathered their manna by affirming: *"Divine Substance cannot be withheld from me now. Divine Substance is the one and only reality in my financial affairs now. Divine*

71

Substance manifests for me here and now in rich, appropriate form as money, money, money, and as rich financial increase."

There is nothing new about this practice. For centuries people have mystically gathered manna by dwelling upon the thought of "substance." This method may seem a new idea to you because it has long been a secret teaching, a secret practice. In the past those who used it found it such a powerful technique that they did not wish to share it with the masses.

Moses spent the first forty years of his life learning this secret teaching in Egypt. He spent another forty years meditating upon it in the Midian Desert. Then during the last forty years of his life, spent in the wilderness, he proved it for himself and his followers. So well did he impart this secret teaching of the prospering power of substance to his followers, that future generations became one of the richest groups of people the world has ever known!

You should not become discouraged if you do not immediately gather as much manna as you would like after learning how. It took Moses, a mental giant, eighty years to do so. But he busily used this secret method, as his needs arose, every step of the way and prospered. You can too!

WHY GATHERING MANNA WAS NECESSARY

After their deliverance from Egyptian bondage, the Hebrews arrived in the wilderness and camped at an oasis where they found twelve wells of water. Since there was no food, Moses inquired of Jehovah how he was to feed the hungry Hebrews. Jehovah replied, "I will rain bread from heaven for you and the people shall go out and gather a day's portion every day." (Exodus 16:4) The Hebrews called this bread "manna."

It looked like a dew or frost, and it had the taste of a wafer made from honey. Each person was instructed to gather as much as he wished daily for six days of each week. On the sixth day, he was instructed to gather enough for his needs on the seventh day too, since no manna appeared on the Sabbath.

Those who gathered little had enough to meet their needs. Those who gathered much had none left over. Each person was free to gather according to his needs and desires. (Exodus 16:16, 18)

During their forty years in the wilderness, the Hebrews daily gathered their manna. Later, upon entering the Promised Land, their food was again provided in normal ways. Jehovah explained to Moses why they were to live off manna one day at a time during their wilderness experience: "That I may prove them, whether they will walk in my law or not." (Exodus 16:4)

The Hebrews had been promised a land of their own flowing with milk and honey, a land of lavish abundance, if they would courageously leave Egypt and all its limitation. But for centuries they had been enslaved by the Egyptians and had believed that the Egyptians were the source of their supply. *With increased freedom comes increased responsibility.*

THE PURPOSE OF A FINANCIAL WILDERNESS

In the wilderness they were given a chance to prove
whether they were willing to now look to God as the source
of their supply. They were given an opportunity to prove
whether they were willing to give up their old methods of
working night and day at the hands of cruel taskmasters
for an assured but tiny pittance. They were given an opportunity to go from the outer "hard work" level of prosperity to the inner mentally-creative level of prosperity.

In their wilderness experiences, the Hebrews were learning to release old ways of living and old methods of work.
They were being shown new ways of producing prosperity
from within out.

After they had fully proved their willingness to depend
upon God as the source of their supply one day at a time,
after they had proved that the substance He provided them
on the sixth day was also sufficient to carry them through
the seventh day, or a non-productive period, then they were
freed from their wilderness wanderings and its one-day-at-
a-time financial existence.

THE LAVISH ABUNDANCE THAT AWAITED THEM
IN THE PROMISED LAND

*They were destined to enter a land far richer even than
the prosperous Egypt from which they had come.* In their
destined Promised Land, no irrigation would be necessary
to produce corn, olives, or grapes in abundance. It was to

be a land profuse in wheat, barley, vines, figs, pomegranates, and honey. It was to be a land of brooks of water, of fountains and springs which flowed forth from the valleys and hills. It was to be a land of iron and copper. As had been promised, they were destined to eat and be filled. They were destined to bless Jehovah for the rich land and good life they would enjoy there. (Deuteronomy 8)

But first they had to prove—one day at a time—their faith in God as the source of their supply in the wilderness. This experience gave them a firm grasp upon, and a deep understanding of, the true inner laws of supply. After their wilderness wanderings, they would not be overwhelmed to find themselves amid lavish abundance in their Promised Land. Because of their one-day-at-a-time prosperity in the wilderness, they would be far more appreciative of the abundance awaiting them in their Promised Land, and they would be far wiser in its use. The "milk and honey" of the Promised Land, that had been promised them, were symbolic of the peace, prosperity, and spirituality they would enjoy there.

Like the Hebrews of that wilderness era, you must be willing to trust Divine Substance to provide for you just one day at a time, if necessary. When you are, you will find that you always have enough. Even on the seventh day— during those nonproductive periods—you will find that the manna previously gathered is sufficient to carry you through. During such nonproductive periods, you should relax, rest and enjoy the manna already on hand. *It is always enough!* Your practice of trusting Divine Substance in this way leads you into your Promised Land of unlimited supply as soon as you are ready for it, both mentally and emotionally.

HOW A BUSINESSMAN PROSPERED IN HIS
FINANCIAL WILDERNESS

If at times you find yourself having similar wilderness experiences, be not dismayed. You are getting ready for greater abundance than you have ever known before. Your wilderness experience is your divine initiation into the higher laws of prosperity. It is also your great opportunity to prove prosperity's dynamic laws. As you do so, from within outwardly, you become free of much limitation. Instead of laboriously making a living, you find yourself making a satisfying life.

A businessman, who has become financially independent through consistent use of the laws of prosperity, has said that one of the first things he discovered in the process was that he had to be willing to give up everything he had previously gained, before he was ever permanently and satisfyingly prospered.

Like the Hebrews of old, he knew what it was to leave an old way of life and an old method of livelihood and to then pass through a financial wilderness on the way to his Promised Land. In that wilderness period, he found out what it was like to prove God as the source of his supply one day at a time.

This man said he discovered that everyone who has ever been greatly prospered from the use of the inner laws of prosperity has had to be willing to give up everything he had for a while in order to prove God as the source of his supply. He said that it was only after these people were willing to do so that permanent prosperity came to them. Because of the understanding they gained in their wilderness experiences, they were able to accept and maintain the rich blessings that poured forth to them later.

YOUR INITIATION INTO PROSPERITY'S DEEPER LEVELS

If you find yourself in the wilderness gathering manna, which seems miraculously supplied as you need it, you can rejoice and give thanks. You can know that you are being initiated into the deeper levels of prosperity! You are getting ready mentally to accept unlimited supply. You are being freed from all fear of lack. A new understanding of the subject is being given you. You are becoming financially independent on a daily basis.

As you develop a true, permanent prosperity consciousness right where you are, you will then expand into unlimited abundance. The results will not unbalance or overwhelm you. Instead, you will be ready to receive, accept, and wisely use the abundance that comes. You will not make a fortune and then lose it, as have so many. As you receive it, you will keep it.

HOW A MAID BECAME A PROSPEROUS SHOPOWNER AND REGAINED HER HEALTH

1. THE FIRST WAY TO GATHER YOUR MANNA:

Your manna is always something close at hand! You can gather your manna by first using something close at hand to meet your need. Be it ever so humble, when you use what is close at hand, your good will multiply.

A woman arrived in a strange city and decided to look up an acquaintance whom she had not seen for five years. She remembered this acquaintance as a household maid in one of the city's richest homes; this woman was a droopy, bitter complainer. She was never well, never sick, just miserable. She had been a person who constantly griped about how badly life had treated her. Though the visitor hesitated to make contact with such an unpleasant person again, an inward urge compelled her to do so.

She went to the spacious home where this maid had worked five years previously. As she rang the bell, she half expected her old friend to answer the door. Instead a butler appeared, assured her that her former friend still lived there, and invited her inside.

In a few minutes, the previously miserable friend greeted her. She hardly recognized the former maid, now radiantly beautiful. The horn-rimmed glasses were gone. She stood erect, poised, with beautiful hair and complexion.

Startled, the visitor blurted out, "How did you do it? What happened? What is your secret?"

Looking around at the lovely studio in which the former maid now lived she also asked, "Have you struck oil?"

Her lovely friend replied, "You might say that I have struck oil, though not literally."

"What have you done?" asked the insistent visitor.

"I have learned how to gather manna."

Ignoring this mystical remark, the friend said, "When I last saw you five years ago, you were a forlorn semi-invalid living off your employer. Now I find you in radiant health, looking years younger, living here in comfortable surroundings. How did you do it? How did you gather that manna?"

The former maid explained, "Four years ago, I had come to the end. I was in poor health, down and out financially, even dependent upon others for my next meal. One day a friend gave me a book on prosperous thinking to read. As I read that book, it gave me hope for a more abundant way of life. One afternoon, as I was meditating upon some of the prosperous ideas from that book and praying for guidance about how this abundant way of life could be mine the thought came, 'Gather your manna.' "

"Not quite understanding what it meant, I decided to take a walk and think about it. During my walk I found myself standing before a store, looking at beautiful cans of bright paint. I realized how starved my soul was for something bright and beautiful in my surroundings. I felt prompted to go into the store and buy a can of that bright paint. The clerk also talked me into buying a can of paint remover.

"As I hurried home, I wondered what had possessed me to impulsively spend the little money I had. When I entered my room, I saw an old chest of drawers, which I had purchased previously and had forgotten about. Looking at it, I realized it was covered with a hideous imitation mahogany paint; that it had beautiful lines and might even be a valuable antique!

"With the words 'gather your manna' still running through my mind, I went to work with the paint remover. Within a short time, I realized that this chest of drawers was a beautiful, costly antique.

"Later that evening a friend came by to check on my welfare. She knew how low I had been, physically and financially. She exclaimed over the chest of drawers and said she had a friend who had been looking for just this type of antique piece. A sale was quickly made. That night I slept with a check for $250 under my pillow! I felt like a millionaire.

"That was the beginning of gathering my manna. After that, I restored and sold a number of valuable antiques which had been gathering dust for lack of attention. I began to tithe from each sale and my manna just grew and grew. The more I tithed, the faster my income increased. My health also improved. Within these four years I have been able to build up a fine business. I now have my own lovely antique shop, and several competent employees to run it." She had used the good at hand and it had multiplied. You can gather your manna in the same way.

So often people have not gathered their manna, because they have stood back waiting to be divinely delivered from their needs in some spectacular way. Your needs will always be supplied when you begin to use something close at hand. You may wish to begin by asking: *"Divine Substance, show me how to 'gather my manna.' Lead me to the abundance at hand. Show me how to use it, and how to multiply it."*

HOW AN OFFICER MULTIPLIED FOOD FOR
HIS SOLDIERS

2. THE SECOND WAY TO GATHER YOUR MANNA:

You can begin to gather your manna by doing something fearless. A commanding officer was met with the challenge of feeding the hungry soldiers in his camp when there was a scarcity of food. His first thought was to give his men half slices of bread, because of the lack. But they had worked hard and were very hungry.

This commanding officer reasoned that according to the law of supply and demand, these men should have *double* rations, instead of half rations. He did the fearless thing and boldly ordered the officer under his command to *double* the thicknesses of the slices of bread.

Just as this was being done, a wagon loaded with provisions miraculously drove into camp, and there was plenty for all! But this miracle had not occurred until this officer had fearlessly begun to use what was on hand. *As you use fearlessly what you have, it multiplies.*

HOW SHE STRETCHED THE FOOD ON HAND

3. THE THIRD WAY TO GATHER YOUR MANNA:

The act of blessing what is on hand can increase it mightily.

A businesswoman proved this. She was between jobs. Her grocery supplies were so low that the only food she had in the house was a small amount of hamburger, some coffee, and a half carton of cream.

This hungry woman started blessing her pocketbook and financial affairs, but nothing happened. She decided to bless the small amount of food that was left, remembering how Jesus had multiplied the loaves and fishes by taking them in his hands and blessing them. (Matthew 14:19)

She anticipated that, as she blessed the food at hand, more food or the money to purchase more food would come to her somehow. This did not happen, but the power of blessing worked anyway.

After the act of blessing the hamburger, cream and coffee, she used a portion of them for her evening fare. The next day, when she again inspected the food, she realized that there appeared to be just as much there as had been before using a portion of it the previous evening!

That food was like the manna in the wilderness that had been gathered on the sixth day and had lasted through the seventh day, when no more appeared. As she continued to bless what was at hand, it met her needs until more money arrived. Through the continued act of blessing, she secured a job and the crisis passed.

HOW A MERCHANT GATHERED MANNA

Something mysterious happens when you bless the substance at hand. Since all forms of substance are filled with intelligence, those forms of substance which you bless respond to praise by multiplying for you.

A merchant decided to take a vacation. While having a cup of coffee in an all-night restaurant, he met a man who was at a very low ebb financially. As the stranger poured out his story of financial woe to this vacationing merchant, the businessman began to remember the power that blessing has to increase one's supply.

He explained to the stranger that he must follow the advice of Paul to "bless and curse not" all his financial problems. (Romans 12:14) After the stranger opened his wallet and showed the merchant how empty it was, his newfound friend suggested that the man hold his empty wallet in his hands while they joined in blessing it. Together they declared: *"We bless you and bless you with the superabundance of Divine Substance. The Lord is your Shepherd. You shall not want."*

Afterwards, almost in jest, the man opened his wallet again and was startled to find a one dollar bill there! That dollar bill started him on his way to a prosperous new life.

HOW A COLLEGE STUDENT GATHERED MANNA

The ancient people knew how to transmute substance. They did it through the power of blessing, through speaking definite words of increased supply, and through forming mental pictures of the desired supply. There is nothing unusual about gathering one's manna in these ways when there is a need for it.

A young college student knew the power of increase that is connected with the act of blessing. He had spent his allowance and was waiting for more money from home. For several days he constantly blessed his wallet with increased supply there, though he knew there was no money in it.

Finally the money from home arrived. Shortly afterwards he opened his wallet to place some of the cash just received in it. Upon opening the wallet he found a five dollar bill there!

HOW A YOUNG COUPLE GATHERED MANNA

A young couple had taken a long trip and were homeward bound. After buying the last tank of gas that would be needed before arriving home, they counted their money and found they had $2 left. With this money they purchased fruit and other food to eat on their homeward drive, feeling certain there would be no need for further funds.

There would have been none, had a toll bridge not been on their route. In order to pass this toll bridge, they needed 35¢. It seemed nonexistent. Instead of panicking, they realized the necessity for gathering their manna. They began to bless Divine Substance and decreed that it was instantly multiplying so that there was sufficient money to meet this demand.

Upon searching wallets, pocketbooks, pants pockets, and the glove compartment of the car, the 35¢ was miraculously gathered. This young couple continued to bless their substance and they prospered. Later the husband was offered the finest job of his life in an executive position. At that point, they departed from their financial wilderness and went into their Promised Land financially secure.

HOW AN ILL, HUNGRY WOMAN GATHERED MANNA THROUGH PICTURING

A businesswoman was ill. She had been out of work for a number of weeks. She had exhausted her salary, her income from sick leave, her hospitalization insurance payments and her savings account.

One morning she felt in special need of having her apartment freshly cleaned by the maid. She knew that a beautiful, clean apartment would uplift her morale and make her feel better physically. But she hesitated to ask the maid to work that day, since she had no money on hand with which to pay her. Following a strong intuitive feeling, she called the maid anyway, who happily agreed to work.

During the day as the rooms were being cleaned, this businesswoman sat quietly, blessing her financial affairs with rich increase. She pictured her wallet and checkbook as filled with cash. She pictured her refrigerator as filled with food. She mentally increased substance in all phases of her world. This mental act of increase gave her a tremendous sense of well-being and emotional uplift.

As the maid concluded her day's work, this lady opened her pocketbook, thinking she would give the maid a post-dated check. Upon impulse she opened her wallet rather than her checkbook. She was astounded to find a crisp new five dollar bill there, which she thankfully passed on to the maid. A knock was then heard at the door and a relative arrived carrying a large bag of groceries—a gift!

This lady enjoyed a clean apartment and a fine meal that evening. The relative prepared it for her. As she continued to praise, bless and give thanks for Divine Substance in every form, her manna continued to appear until she was able to return to work and to more normal methods of supply. Later she was given a promotion and raise in pay, which relieved her of any further financial strain.

MANNA HAS APPEARED FOR THE AUTHOR

I personally believe that it is possible for substance to multiply and appear in mysterious ways when the need demands it. It has happened to me—as it has to most people—at various times.

On one occasion I opened a dresser drawer and found a one dollar bill there when it was greatly needed. On another occasion, when I needed money, I opened a book I had previously read and found a ten dollar bill between its pages!

Friends of mine recently made a special study of the laws of prosperity. One night they opened a table drawer and found two twenty dollar bills. They are not the type to carelessly place money in table drawers, any more than I am the type to casually place money between the pages of a book.

One should not make it a point to try to demonstrate

prosperity in these dramatic ways when there are more normal ways of supply available. But it is good to know you can gather your manna in such a manner if the circumstances of your life demand it.

WHEN SHE BLESSED ANOTHER'S PROSPERITY SHE ALSO RECEIVED NEW SUPPLY

4. THE FOURTH WAY TO GATHER YOUR MANNA:

Instead of envying another's prosperity, bless it. Blessing another's prosperity opens the way for increased supply to come to you.

Members of a church congregation were quietly collecting a special offering for their minister. The lady in charge of this project kept holding in mind that the final gift for the minister would be a certain figure of several hundred dollars. Everytime anyone gave her money in the amounts of one dollar, five dollars, ten or twenty dollars toward this gift, she would quietly bless it and mentally multiply it to be the final figure being held in mind.

Not only did the final amount she desired for the minister's gift arrive as the offerings were gathered, but, as she blessed these gifts, in a totally unforeseen way she personally received a gift of money in the same amount that had been given the minister! By blessing someone else's prosperity, she had attracted her own.

You can, too. Try it.

HOW $2,000 CAME TO THEM TO PAY THEIR DEBTS

5. THE FIFTH WAY TO GATHER YOUR MANNA:

Since words are creative, you can gather your manna through speaking forth definite, rich words of supply, even in the face of apparent lack.

A housewife from Arizona wrote:

"My husband and I declared aloud together every day for several weeks these words, *'We are guided into our true place with, the true people and with the true prosperity now.'* The results? We got an unexpected cash refund from the government of $2,000! Real manna from heaven.

"We also found as we continued to declare prosperity statements every day that within a couple of months we were able to pay off all of our long-term debts. We even had a cash surplus every payday after all bills were paid. The only explanation to this sudden change in our financial affairs from indebtedness to abundance is that of taking up the practice of saying prosperity statements faithfully for a few minutes every day. That practice has proved to be the best investment we've ever made. Anybody can prosper who does this."

HOW HE SOLD HIS CAR AT THE LAST MINUTE

A mother wrote from Texas:

"My son's orders to report to the United States Navy came sooner than we had expected. He had to sell his car, and he needed to get the rest of his affairs in order. He had waited until the weekend just before he was to leave to advertise the sale of his car in the local paper. Nothing happened in response to that ad on Saturday. There was not a single call.

"On Sunday morning, we sat down and declared aloud together: *'The all-powerful right action of God is at work in this situation for the buyer, the seller, and the holder of the car title. The perfect sale now takes place quickly and in peace.'* By noon, the car was sold at the right price to someone who seemed happy to get it. The buyer even arranged to send the check to the bank, who held the title, paying off the loan in my son's name. He wrote another check to my son for the balance. We were amazed how quickly this matter was settled when we spoke prosperous words together about it."

HOW TO GET OUT OF A FINANCIAL WILDERNESS FOREVER

Do not criticize your wilderness experiences. Instead, make the best of them. Affirm that good things are happening to you. Praise, bless and use what is at hand. *You always have in your immediate midst whatever is needed to begin gathering your manna.* As you use it fearlessly, your good will multiply in countless ways.

Speak forth definite prosperous decrees: *"As I bless my manna and fearlessly use it, it now multiplies. Lord, I do give thee thanks for the abundance that is now mine!"* Then praise and bless the prosperity of others.

In all these ways you can gather your manna—that sustenance that seems miraculously supplied in time of need. As you gather your manna, you should then prepare for the overflow of prosperity that awaits you as you move out of a financial wilderness into the expanded prosperity consciousness known as your Promised Land.

In that expanded prosperity consciousness you, too, will doubtless "eat and be full" as did the Hebrews of old.

So give thanks to God for all that you have learned in your financial wilderness, because those experiences were preparing you for the vast blessings of your rich Promised Land!

A PROSPERITY MEDITATION FOR
GATHERING YOUR MANNA

"WHEN I FIND MYSELF IN A FINANCIAL WILDERNESS, IT IS BECAUSE I AM PREPARED FOR A GREATER ABUNDANCE THAN I HAVE EVER KNOWN BEFORE. MY WILDERNESS EXPERIENCE IS MY DIVINE INITIATION INTO THE HIGHER LEVELS OF SUPPLY. I AM BEING FREED FROM ALL FEAR OF LACK. AS I LOOK TO GOD FOR GUIDANCE AND SUPPLY, I AM BECOMING FINANCIALLY INDEPENDENT ON A DAILY BASIS.

"I CAN GATHER MY MANNA BY FIRST USING SOMETHING CLOSE AT HAND TO MEET MY NEED. BE IT EVER SO HUMBLE, WHEN I USE WHAT IS CLOSE AT HAND, MY GOOD MULTIPLIES. I CAN BEGIN TO GATHER MY MANNA BY DOING SOMETHING FEARLESS. THE ACT OF BLESSING WHAT IS ON HAND INCREASES IT MIGHTILY. SOMETHING MYSTERIOUS HAPPENS WHEN I BLESS THE SUBSTANCE AT HAND. INSTEAD OF ENVYING ANOTHER'S PROSPERITY, I OPEN THE WAY FOR INCREASED SUPPLY TO COME TO ME. SINCE WORDS ARE CREATIVE, I CAN GATHER MY MANNA THROUGH SPEAKING FORTH DEFINITE, RICH WORDS OF SUPPLY, EVEN IN THE FACE OF LACK. MY MANNA IS ALWAYS SOMETHING CLOSE AT HAND, AND I ALWAYS HAVE IN MY IMMEDIATE MIDST WHATEVER IS NEEDED TO BEGIN GATHERING MY MANNA. AS I BLESS THE MANNA CLOSE AT HAND AND FEARLESSLY USE IT, IT MULTIPLIES. LORD, I DO GIVE THANKS FOR THE ABUNDANCE THAT IS MINE NOW!"

SUMMARY

1. The word "manna" means "any needed sustenance that seems miraculously supplied." "Manna" is that substance that comes to us out of the heavenly realms of the mind. We gather it and "eat" it, basically through prosperity decrees.

2. One of the quickest ways to gather your manna is by calling on Divine Substance through repeated prosperity decrees spoken aloud. This stirs up the wealth of the universe and causes it to be manifested for you in appropriate form.

3. After their deliverance from Egyptian bondage, the Hebrews were fed in the wilderness with manna from heaven, which they gathered daily for six days. On the sixth day they gathered enough for their needs on the seventh day when no manna appeared.

4. Those who gathered little had enough to meet their needs. Those who gathered much had none left over. Each person was free to gather according to his needs and desires.

5. Through this experience the Hebrews learned to look to God as the source of their supply. They were freed from the "hard-work" methods they had used in Egypt.

6. This experience gave them a firm grasp upon, and a deep understanding of, the true inner laws of supply. Later, when they found themselves amid lavish abundance in their Promised Land, they would not be overwhelmed by it.

7. You must be willing to trust Divine Substance to provide for you just one day at a time, if necessary. When you are, you will find that you always have enough. In the midst of such experiences, be not dismayed. You are getting ready for greater abundance than you have ever known!

8. How to gather your manna:
   a) You can gather your manna by using something close at hand. When you use what is close at hand, your good multiplies.
   b) You can begin to gather your manna by doing something fearless. As you use what you have fearlessly, it multiplies.
   c) You can gather your manna through the act of blessing what is on hand. This increases it mightily.
   d) Instead of envying another's prosperity, bless it. This opens the way for increased supply to come to you.
   e) Since words are creative, you can gather your manna through speaking forth definite, rich words of supply, even in the face of apparent lack.

9. Do not criticize your wilderness experiences. They are forcing you to become financially independent on a daily basis. You are being initiated into deeper levels of supply.

10. You always have in your immediate midst whatever is needed to begin gathering your manna. As you use it fearlessly, your good will multiply in countless ways. You will be on your way to permanent prosperity.

YOUR SECRET WEAPONS
FOR PROSPERITY

— Chapter 5 —

Your secret weapons for prosperity are symbolized in two incidents in the life of Moses in the desert: One occurred early in his wilderness wanderings; the other occurred much later. From these two events you learn how to quietly claim your good:

First. In the face of opposition.

Second. In the midst of hard conditions.

Soon after getting out of Egypt, crossing the Red Sea and entering the wilderness, the Hebrews were warred upon by a desert tribe known as the Amaleks.

The word "Amalek" means "warlike," "dwellers in the valley." The Amaleks were plunderers. They symbolize the feelings of depression and discouragement that confront you when challenges arise that plunder your emotions. Moses overcame these warlike plunderers and you can, too.

YOUR FIRST SECRET WEAPON FOR PROSPERITY

We all have .to meet the Amaleks. They are those warring forces that appear as problems and challenges. *There is nothing negative about having to overcome problems or to meet challenges in life. They are experiences in growth. If you are growing inwardly as well as outwardly, there will be Amaleks along the way.* As you meet them in a certain way, they can cause you to grow into your expanded good and to prosper.

You can begin to overcome the Amaleks when you realize that there are two kinds:

First. There are the problems (Amaleks) that result from your own negative thoughts, words and actions. When you begin to think, speak, and act constructively upon the belief in omnipresent good, you overcome this type of Amalek either quickly or at least progressively.

Second. There are also the problems (Amaleks) that result—not from the negative thoughts, words or actions in life—but from the mere necessity for growth. By having to meet this type of problem with constructive thoughts, words and actions, you grow out of the problem into an increased understanding. In the process you have gotten your roots implanted deep in the invisible realm of substance, which gives you a firm foundation for experiencing all of life's blessings in ever-increasing degrees.

When you use the Prosperity Commandments that are described in the next chapter, and the other prosperous attitudes pointed out in this book, you begin to expand your consciousness. Problems that seem as difficult and as warlike as the Amaleks may appear on your path. If so, *they are blessings in disguise.*

By steadfastly following the formula that Moses used with the Amaleks, you can overcome your "dwellers in the valley." But you must know them for what they are: They are not enemies but friends because they are problems in growth—nothing else.

Plato knew this when he spoke of the two kinds of blindness that affect mankind:

First. There is the blindness of going from light into darkness. This is the first kind of problem you have, caused by negative thinking.

Second. There is the blindness of coming out of the darkness into the light. These are the problems in growth.

As you take up the use of the prosperous attitudes described in this book, you may encounter the "growth problems" that accompany all who are coming out of darkness into the light. These are not problems, though their guise is impressive. They are times of soul-expansion into the light of increased understanding and use of one's mind powers.

Although these two kinds of problems look alike, they are as different as day and night. *Knowledge of this is your first secret weapon for prosperity and success.*

THIS PROSPERITY SECRET WORKED FOR AUTHOR

In reflecting upon my own evolving progress over the past thirty years, I can see now how often I have had to meet the Amaleks in these two guises:

That of going from light into darkness, and that of being blinded when coming out of the darkness into the light. It is good finally to know why some problems were resolved quickly through the use of constructive thinking, while other problems tenaciously hung on for long periods, no matter how much prayer and constructive thinking were applied to them. I can now "pronounce them good" since they were problems that forced me to grow into the light of increased understanding through the use of my mind powers.

When that happened to a sufficient degree, I was then freed of the problems of long standing, sometimes suddenly and in dramatic ways. The freedom and dominion, the beauty and abundance, that have come into my life in recent years have more than compensated for the many drab and dreary years of my earlier life. Because I had so little to work with in the beginning of my journey from darkness into the light, I am convinced that anyone can do it if they persist. Sooner or later the "plunderers" have to flee!

YOUR SECOND SECRET WEAPON FOR PROSPERITY

When Moses learned that the Amaleks were planning to attack the Hebrews, he sent Joshua and his men out to meet the Amaleks. He told Joshua he would stand on a hill and hold up his hands. As long as Moses' hands were uplifted, it indicated that Joshua and the Hebrews were winning. When Moses' hands were let down, it would mean that the Amaleks were winning. By watching the position of Moses' hands, Joshua could determine the course of the battle.

Moses took Aaron and Hur with him to the top of the hill. When Moses tired of holding up his hands, Aaron and Hur assisted by holding them up for him. They helped Moses keep his hands uplifted until nightfall, and Joshua was able to overcome the Amaleks in battle.

Moses with outstretched hands is perhaps the first example of the symbolic use of the cross in the Bible. The cross was a spiritual symbol employed by people from early times. It was found among the ancient people of India, China, Egypt, Greece, and Mexico as a symbol of divine intervention in the affairs of mankind. Moses' upstretched hands formed a marvelous picture of the prayerful bringing of divine power into human affairs. Of course, the hands of Moses had already become a symbol of divine help to the Hebrews. Moses' outstretched hands had brought freedom from the plagues, a divided sea, freedom from slavery, delivery from hunger and thirst in the wilderness. Now his hands brought power and victory. That certain people have the spiritual power to protect and help others in time of need is a central theme in the religious experiences of mankind.

Aaron was the brother of Moses. His name means "strength." Hur was the brother-in-law of Moses. His name means "affirmation." The hands of Moses symbolize the executive power of the mind. When the mind is uplifted, you overcome. When the mind is downcast, you are inclined to lose in life's battles.

You may often tire of trying to be positive in the face of problems, just as Moses' hands got tired of being uplifted in the face of enemy forces. The hands symbolize our use of the five basic ideas in Divine Mind: life, love, wisdom, power, and substance. (See chapter on *Strength* in my book, *The Healing Secrets of the Ages*.[1])

Like Moses, you always have Hur or the power of positive words to help you. Like Moses, you always have Aaron or the mind power of strength to uplift you. You can call on your Hur and Aaron mind powers to help hold up your thinking until the battle is won, and the overcoming has been made.

After victory with the Amaleks, Moses built an altar, offering prayers and financial sacrifices to Jehovah in appreciation for answered prayer. Later, when he recounted to his father-in-law, Jethro, all that Jehovah had done, Jethro also showed his appreciation by giving sacrifices and offerings to Jehovah—another act of spiritual and financial thanksgiving to God. (Exodus 17 and 18) Over and over the Hebrews "sealed" their blessings of victory and answered prayer with the spiritual and financial acts of thanksgiving. (See Chapter 8) They did not take their blessings for

---

1. Catherine Ponder, *The Healing Secrets of the Ages* (Marina del Rey, CA: DeVorss & Co., rev. ed. 1983).

granted. *When the battle has been won, don't forget to give thanks, both spiritually and financially.*

HOW YOU CAN USE THIS SECRET WEAPON

If you seem unable to get an uplifted viewpoint, talk confidentially with a positive thinker—a friend, relative, counselor or minister whom you can trust. They can help you achieve the lift needed to look down on your problems, rather than up at them. Reading and studying along inspirational and self-help lines, listening to inspirational tapes, attending uplifting lectures, seminars, and church services accomplish this for many people.

Although my schedule no longer allows me the luxury of counseling with people on an individual basis, I thoroughly enjoyed doing so for many years. I have been repeatedly amazed at the delightful results that occurred from talking first about the problem the way it appeared to be, then discussing it from the standpoint of what universal good is to be found in the experience, and finally how to extract that good from it. The process was called by old-time-metaphysicians "divinely reasoning together." This method, coupled with our joint verbal affirmative prayers, usually brought the needed viewpoints and results.

A letter recently arrived which read: "Two years ago, I came to see you about a divorce suit. You prayed with me and helped me to change my point of view. The result? The judgment has now come in and I have been awarded a quarter of a million dollars! This is a fantastic settlement under the circumstances."

THE SUCCESS POWER OF PRAYER PARTNERS

Another method that has helped me personally is this:
For the past twenty-five years I have had secret prayer partners who have acted as a Hur or an Aaron in my life. These prayer partners have helped me hold up my hands, or hold up divine ideas of good, in the midst of challenging experiences. As they used positive decrees with me, their prayer power, aligned with my own, gave the added strength needed to meet those challenging experiences victoriously, both for myself and for others.

While in the business world in North Carolina, my prayer partners at various times were an office maid, and one of the town's leading matrons. Later in Alabama, a housewife, a career woman, and a business executive were my prayer partners. In Texas a housewife was my prayer partner for more than ten years. Members of my family have acted as prayer partners, too, over the years. (See my book, *Pray and Grow Rich.*[2])

Everyone should have a Hur and an Aaron in their lives! I count my prayer partners among my greatest blessings. The staunch support they have given me, and the many affirmations they have spoken with me over the last twenty-five years have helped to open the way for all the blessings

2. Catherine Ponder, *The Dynamic Laws of Prayer*, formerly *Pray and Grow Rich* (Marina del Rey, CA: DeVorss & Co., rev. ed. 1986).

I now enjoy in my life—blessings which I do not take for granted because they were absent from my life for so long.

HOW AN ENGLISH SHOPKEEPER MET THE MORTGAGE PAYMENT

There is nothing new about this success technique. People have been proving the victorious power of words for centuries.

Your words (Hur) are your own to do with as you please. Your words are the weapons with which you cut out your destiny.

A woman in England was facing the Amaleks in the form of a financial challenge. She had an antique shop in what she described as a "wee village" in southern England. She had been in the process of buying this antique shop when the former owner of it passed on. His heirs did not want this mortgaged property. They wanted to settle the estate. They told the lady she must pay the balance she owed on the shop right away. In English pounds the amount needed was equivalent to several thousand American dollars.

Her banker would not loan her the money. She talked with a friend who suggested she call on the power of this affirmative statement: *"All financial doors are now open to me. All financial channels are now free to me. The money required now appropriately comes to me quickly and in peace."*

Her prospering words proved to be her secret weapon for success. As the deadline for payment approached, a man walked into her antique shop. He browsed and they talked.

He was the manager of the other bank in this "wee village." She told him of her financial need, and at his suggestion, she transferred her accounts to his bank. That bank then quickly loaned her the money to pay off the mortgage on her shop.

HOW THIS SECRET WEAPON CURED A HOPELESS HEALTH PROBLEM

As you dwell upon good words and speak them forth (Hur), this gives you the strength (Aaron) to hold onto the thought of good until it appears. Like Moses, you never have to hold up your thinking alone.

Through knowledge of this one success principle, you now know enough to change the course of your life! One affirmation, activated and made real in your affairs, is worth more than dozens of books read, lectures attended, or advice sought.

When you begin to hold up your thinking through affirmations, they give you the strength "to keep on keeping on" until the breaking forth of good in the situation. That good often comes to you through people and events that were unforeseen to you.

A businesswoman spoke to a friend of her sister, who had experienced a marvelous recovery. For years this sister had been "almost dead with arthritis." She had been subjected to numerous drugs and special treatments to effect a cure, but had found no relief.

The friend asked, "What is the secret of your sister's healing? I thought she had an incurable case of arthritis."

The businesswoman replied that her sister's recovery dated from the day she began to affirm life and healing for herself. She decided to practice looking for the good in her fellow workers, especially in those who had been difficult. She placed their names on her prayer list and beheld them growing into the Light daily.

Her secret weapon for success worked beautifully. It took several years of persistent effort to effect a complete healing, but there was improvement from the start. This encouraged her to persist. She is now free from pain. She has received a promotion in her job. She owns a new car and has moved into her own lovely apartment. She has also just come into a sizeable inheritance! Her sister said, "You would hardly recognize her, she has changed so much. Her life has vastly improved in just a few short years."

HOW SHE FREED HER FATHER FROM PRISON

Not only can you hold up your own thinking through affirming good things for yourself, but you can help others win their battles in life by holding up your thinking about them. When you see others facing challenges, you can help them whether they know it or not.

There once was a daughter whose aged father had been in prison for five years. He had been convicted of a crime he had not committed. The finest lawyers had tried to obtain his freedom to no avail.

One day this daughter decided to *mentally* give her father his freedom. She said to him mentally, "Here is your freedom. It is God's gift. Wake up and take it. Get up and go forth. You are free." Within a few days through a swift series of events, this man was released from prison and completely exonerated from the crime for which he had been accused. Nothing had happened until words of freedom had been affirmed for him *mentally* first.

Mentally speak to other people and give them the good they long for. Say to them: *"Here is your health. Here is your freedom. Here is your prosperity. Here is your happiness. It is God's gift to you. Wake up and take it. Get up and go forth. You are free. You are abundantly blessed."* The gratifying results of this practice can amaze and delight you!

HOW A MOTHER HEALED HER SON OF DRINKING

A mother was concerned about her son, who drank heavily and who was leading a life of degradation. She had tried to reason with him, but without success. Finally she began to pray for him daily. In her prayers she mentally gave him his freedom as she said: *"I release you, loose you; I let go and let God heal you in His own way."*

One night a few weeks later her son came home and said, "Mother, I am tired of leading this kind of life. I am through with it." He never drank again.

HOW HE WAS HEALED OF MISTREATING
AN EMPLOYEE

When you hold up others in your thinking through affirmations about them, you impart to them the inner strength they need to overcome their difficulties!

A clerk at a military base was mistreated by her boss until she started praying for him. He quickly felt her uplifted thoughts and they became good friends.

HOW SHE BROUGHT ABOUT RECONCILIATION OF TWO FRIENDS

By holding up those who seem difficult with your affirmative thoughts and words, you help them to overcome whatever has made them difficult.

During a seven-week Lenten period, a lady decided to pray for two of her neighbors. They had not spoken to each other for several years. Daily she blessed them and pictured them in the Light. It worked. One day just prior to Easter, she looked out of her window and saw these women happily chatting with each other as though nothing had ever been wrong between them.

YOUR THIRD SECRET WEAPON FOR PROSPERITY

From an incident which occurred later in Moses' life, we find a third secret weapon for prosperity and success: that of meeting hard conditions victoriously. It is a re-emphasis of the first secret weapon for prosperity described earlier in this chapter. (The same success principles were often repeated in new guises in the Bible to emphasize their importance.)

In the Desert of Zin, there was no water. The thirsty Hebrews again complained:

"Why have you brought us into the wilderness to die? Why did you make us leave Egypt? There are no seeds, figs, vines or pomegranates. Neither is there any any water to drink."

(Numbers 20:4, 5)

When there was a need, Moses always asked for specific guidance and Jehovah always gave it:

"Take the rod, gather the assembly together, and speak unto the rock before their eyes, that it shall give forth water."

(Numbers 20:8)

Earlier in their wilderness wanderings, the Hebrews had needed water and Moses had obtained it for them by following an outer course of action. (Exodus 15:25; 17:6) This time Jehovah gave fresh new instructions about how to solve the same problem. He specified that Moses was to *speak* to the rock. But Moses did not listen. He struck the rock twice and water gushed forth. The temporary need was met, but Moses got a long-term reaction for his disobedience:

"Because ye believed me not, ye shall not bring this congregation into the land which I have given them."
(Numbers 20:12)

It sounds like harsh punishment for one act of disobedience. But the working of the law is impersonal. Disobedience to the law often brings a similar reaction for us, too.

If we ask for guidance but do not follow it, we may have long periods of non-demonstration, so that our Promised Land of increased good seems to evade us.

HOW TO RESOLVE HARD CONDITIONS IN YOUR LIFE

Most people in the world today are trying to dissolve the hard conditions in their lives by striking out at them with force. Earlier in Moses' wilderness experience, he had solved the problem of water by following an *outer* course of action. Now, much later, he had outgrown that method. Instead of using outer force, he was ready to use *inner* force.

If there are hard conditions in your life that haven't yielded to your use of prosperous thinking, you may have been using an old method that has worked for you in the past, but which will not work for you now because growth has taken place.

Ask for guidance. *Then follow that guidance, no matter what it is.* When Moses refused to follow a new method for solving an old problem, he kept himself out of the Promised Land. You may have, too.

You cannot live off past realizations. Once when I was trying to find a new way to solve an old problem, I went to my favorite inspirational books. I reviewed all the methods that had worked for me in the past. I studied all of my favorite Bible passages. This time nothing worked. The rocky problem loomed as big as ever.

One day, after asking for guidance, I was led to an inspirational booklet that had been in my library for years.

Upon opening its unfamiliar pages, I found just the ideas needed. A great sense of peace came over me as I put them to work and got results. In less than a week, the old hard condition began to crack up, then it yielded completely. But only after I discarded past realizations and former methods, and asked for fresh new guidance.

HOW A KINDERGARTEN TEACHER IMPROVED HER WORLD WITH WORDS

If you haven't gotten into your Promised Land, you may have been trying to force your way in, when all you needed to do was to speak words describing the result you wanted. You can keep yourself out of your Promised Land through sheer carelessness and neglect.

The law of Eternal Good is mighty to accomplish worth-while results in your life, but it must be spoken into activity. It must be described in words. You can release your good into action through your good words.

A kindergarten teacher had had problem children in her kindergarten. At the beginning of a new year she purposely said often to her family and friends, "I have nothing but angels in my kindergarten this year. They are *all* perfect angels."

For the first time, she had no problem children. On cold days her students were happy to stay inside with quiet games, whereas in the past there had always been those who had been restless, noisy and had created havoc. That teach-

ing year proved to be the happiest in her long career—
thanks to her use of good words.

HOW A BUSINESSWOMAN MOVED INTO A BETTER JOB

When a professional woman found herself surrounded by
uncongenial co-workers, she deliberately began to say every
day, "I have come into an innumerable company of angels
now." The people on her job did not change, but she was
soon offered a job in another state. Her new co-workers were
happy to have her and they showed it every day. She
thought, "These are my angels."

HOW TO SPEAK TO YOUR ROCK

The success secret connected with Moses' episode with
the rock is that *you can dissolve hard conditions in your
life with words*. There is tremendous magic even in ordinary words. People have often talked themselves into the
grave through their use of ordinary words like "I feel bad,"
"I am so sick," "I don't think I'm going to make it." "I
inherited my bad health. It runs in the family."

*The power that your words have upon your body and
upon your financial affairs is nothing short of fantastic.*
Optimistic people, strickened with illness, have talked themselves back to health. Financially stricken people have talked
their way back to prosperity. Because of the creative power
of words, you need no longer hesitate to *speak* to rocky conditions. They *will* respond.

HOW A LANDLORD RENTED ROOMS SUCCESSFULLY

A landlord had several vacant rooms that needed to be rented. Because it was an off-season for tourists, there were hundreds of similar rooms for rent in his town. After having exhausted the usual methods of renting his rooms, he decided to use an unusual method. Walking through the empty rooms he declared over and over in a loud voice: *"It is right that these rooms should be rented now. I declare that each room now draws to it those people who need it, who are looking for it, and who are ready to rent it for cash."*

This time when he placed an ad in the newspaper, within two days all of his vacant rooms were rented, even though local landlords continued to complain about vacancies. When he stopped talking *about* the rock and spoke directly *to* it, it dissolved.

HOW A TEENAGER MADE NEW FRIENDS

A teenager desired new friends. Nothing happened until she spoke these words: *"I walk in the charmed circle of God's love, and I am divinely irresistible to my highest good now."* Within a week, she was invited to several parties where she met the kind of friends she had longed for.

RENAME YOUR DIFFICULTIES

If the hard conditions in your life include difficult people, don't strike out at them. Instead of trying to make them over, rename them! To unpleasant or uncooperative people in your world, rename them with good names. Describe them as "cooperative, helpful, truthful, courteous, harmonious." Those in your world will either "shape up or ship out." Your words will move undesirable people out of your orbit and bring the right kind into it.

Say: *"You may have meant it for evil, but God means this experience between us for good. I rename you good. I rename this relationship good. Only good shall come from this relationship. You have come into my life for good and for good only!"*

Every positive statement you make turns on lights in your world. Every negative statement you make turns them off.

HOW A WIFE SAVED HER MARRIAGE WITH WORDS

The words that most often change your life are the ordinary, casual, simple words you speak in daily conversation. They have fantastic power.

A lovely young wife confided to her closest friend, "My husband has asked for a divorce. I have known for some time he was not happy but I've tried to do everything to please him. He says he is in love with someone else."

The friend said, "If you still love him, call on the power of words to make things right. Say everyday: *'My home is a haven of love, peace and harmony now.'* Then act as though it were so, regardless."

It was not easy for this wife to speak or act in this way, but she persevered. Every night she continued to prepare dinner for two, although her husband did not appear. In the face of inharmony between them she continued to say, *"My home is a haven of love, peace and harmony now."*

This rocky condition did not yield easily. One day, many months later, a lovely young lady knocked at her door. "I am here to ask you to give up your husband. He doesn't love you any more. He wants to marry me."

The young wife's heart beat rapidly as she prayed for the right words. Instead of inviting the unwanted visitor in for an inharmonious confrontation she replied quietly, "I don't believe that. Will you please excuse me? I am very busy."

As she closed the door, it was as though she had confronted the hard condition firmly for the last time. By saying "No" to it, she closed the door on it forever. Mentioning this episode to no one, she continued preparing dinner each night for her absent husband. She continued to speak words of harmony for their marriage.

A few nights later her husband came home for dinner! He said, "Is there anything I can do to help?" She put him to work. Later that evening as peace prevailed between them he said, "You may not realize it but you have saved me from the worst mistake of my life."

HOW TO CLEAR ROCKY CONDITIONS OUT OF YOUR LIFE

When there is great need or a hard condition in your life, meet it on its own terms—by emphatically speaking good words about it. Be deliberate, definite, positive and persistent. This method has worked for thousands of others and it will clear rocky conditions out of your life, too!

A MEDITATION FOR INVOKING
YOUR SECRET WEAPONS FOR PROSPERITY

"I CAN KEEP MYSELF OUT OF MY PROMISED LAND THROUGH SHEER CARELESSNESS AND NEGLECT. IF I HAVEN'T GOTTEN INTO MY PROMISED LAND, I MAY HAVE BEEN TRYING TO FORCE MY WAY IN WHEN ALL I NEEDED TO DO WAS TO SPEAK WORDS DESCRIBING IT.

"MY WORDS ARE THE WEAPONS WITH WHICH I CAN CUT OUT MY DESTINY. AS I DWELL UPON GOOD WORDS AND SPEAK THEM FORTH, THIS GIVES ME THE STRENGTH TO HOLD ONTO THE THOUGHT OF GOOD UNTIL IT APPEARS. ONE AFFIRMATION, ACTIVATED AND MADE REAL IN MY AFFAIRS, IS WORTH MORE THAN DOZENS OF BOOKS READ, LECTURES ATTENDED, OR ADVICE SOUGHT. EVERY POSITIVE STATEMENT I SPEAK TURNS ON LIGHTS IN MY WORLD. EVERY NEGATIVE STATEMENT I MAKE TURNS THEM OFF. THE WORDS I SPEAK IN DAILY CONVERSATION HAVE FANTASTIC POWER, TOO.

"THE LAW OF ETERNAL GOOD IS MIGHTY TO ACCOMPLISH WORTHWHILE RESULTS IN MY LIFE, BUT IT MUST BE SPOKEN INTO ACTIVITY. IT MUST BE DESCRIBED IN WORDS. I CAN RELEASE MY GOOD INTO ACTION THROUGH MY GOOD WORDS: *'God means this experience for good. This experience has come into my life for good only. So I pronounce it good, and only good shall come from it.'* THE POWER THAT MY WORDS HAVE UPON MY MIND, BODY AND FINANCIAL AFFAIRS IS NOTHING SHORT OF FANTASTIC.

"WHEN THERE IS A GREAT NEED OR A HARD CONDITION IN MY LIFE, I MEET IT ON ITS OWN TERMS. I EMPHATICALLY SPEAK GOOD WORDS ABOUT IT. THIS CLEARS ROCKY CONDITIONS OUT OF MY LIFE FOREVER. GOOD WORDS NOW MOVE ME INTO MY PROMISED LAND WHERE I BELONG."

SUMMARY

1. Your *first* secret weapon for prosperity is this: We all have to meet the Amaleks, as did the Hebrews early in their wilderness wanderings. The word "Amalek" means "warlike." The Amaleks are those warring forces that appear as problems and challenges in our lives. There is nothing negative about having to overcome problems or to meet challenges in life. They are experiences in growth. If you are growing inwardly as well as progressing outwardly, there will be Amaleks along the way.

2. You can begin to overcome the Amaleks when you realize there are two kinds:

   First. There are the problems (Amaleks) that result from your own negative thoughts, words and actions. When you begin to think, speak and act constructively, you overcome this type of Amalek either quickly or progressively.

   Second. There are also the problems (Amaleks) that result from the mere necessity for growth. By meeting this type of problem with constructive thoughts, words and actions, you grow out of the problem into an increased understanding, and you gain a firm foundation for experiencing life's blessings in ever-increasing degrees. Thus the Amaleks become blessings in disguise.

3. Plato spoke of the two kinds of blindness that affect mankind:

   First. There is the blindness of going from light into darkness. This is the first kind of problem you have, caused by negative thinking.

Second. There is the blindness of coming out of the darkness into the light. These are problems in growth, times of soul-expansion. Their solution may seem to take longer.

4. When Moses learned that the Amaleks were planning to attack the Hebrews, he sent Joshua and his men out to meet the Amaleks. He told Joshua he would stand on a hill and hold up his hands. As long as Moses' hands were uplifted, it indicated that Joshua and the Hebrews were winning. When Moses' hands were let down, it would mean that the Amaleks were winning. By watching the position of Moses' hands, Joshua could determine the course of the battle.

5. Moses took Aaron and Hur with him to the top of the hill. When Moses tired of holding up his hands, Aaron and Hur assisted by holding them up for him. They helped Moses keep his hands uplifted until nightfall, and Joshua was able to overcome the Amaleks.

6. The name "Aaron" means "strength." The name "Hur" means "affirmation." The hands of Moses symbolize the executive power of the mind. When the mind is uplifted, you overcome. When the mind is downcast, you are inclined to lose life's battles.

7. Your *second* secret weapon for prosperity is this: Like Moses, you always have Hur or the power of positive words to help you. Like Moses, you always have Aaron or the mind power of strength to uplift you. These two powers can help hold up your thinking until the overcoming is made.

8. Your words (Hur) are your own to do with as you please. Your words are the weapons with which you cut out your destiny. Through knowledge of this one success principle, you now know enough to change the course of your life!

9. Later in Moses' life, we find a *third* secret weapon for prosperity: You can dissolve hard conditions in your life through words. In the Desert of Zin, when there was no water, Jehovah instructed Moses to *speak* to the rock. Instead Moses struck the rock as he had done previously, and water gushed forth. But Moses got a long-term reaction for his disobedience. He was not allowed to enter the Promised Land. If we ask for guidance, but do not follow it, we may have long periods of non-demonstration, so that our Promised Land of increased good seems to evade us. Instead, ask for guidance, then follow it, no matter what it is.

10. You can keep yourself out of your Promised Land through sheer carelessness and neglect. If you haven't gotten into your Promised Land, you may have been trying to force your way in when all you needed to do was to speak words describing the result you wanted.

THE PROSPERITY COMMANDMENTS

— Chapter 6 —

A clubwoman said proudly to a visiting Rabbi, "One of my relatives came over on the Mayflower, and another of my relatives signed the Declaration of Independence."

The Rabbi coolly replied, "And one of *my* relatives signed the Ten Commandments."

Moses has often been described as the emancipator of his people from Egyptian bondage. He was that, but he was also much more. As stated previously, Moses' mission was a prosperity mission! When you realize this, you can see why the Ten Commandments are powerful "prosperity commandments" for you today.

Let us review why Moses' mission was a prosperity mission.

The Hebrews had gone to Egypt because of their need for supply during a seven-year famine, when one of their kinsmen, Joseph, was Prime Minister of Egypt. Not only did Joseph save them from starvation but he also arranged for them to remain in Egypt in comparative comfort.

As long as Joseph remained in power, his kinsmen were welcomed in Egypt. But at his passing, the Egyptians began to resent the Hebrews, thinking of them as parasites. Egyptian slavery and bondage followed for the Hebrews.

At this point, the mission of Moses was to help the Hebrews realize that God was the source of their supply; that they did not have to remain in bondage to a foreign power for their prosperity; that, indeed, they could enjoy prosperous living in their own Promised Land—"a land flowing with milk and honey."

After leading them out of Egypt, Moses proved to the Hebrews that God could supply their needs one day at a time, with manna from heaven, and with water from the rock. In spite of his proof to them that God was an all-providing Father, they were not happy. Even though they had been slaves in Egypt, at least they had been assured of a reasonable degree of prosperity, they lamented.

As most of us do at times, they wanted to settle for the lesser blessings of life, rather than demonstrate faith in God as their supply, thereby claiming unlimited good in their lives. The Hebrews continually criticized and opposed Moses in the wilderness, and Moses turned to God, asking for guidance in leading these rebellious people to their rich Promised Land.

To help Moses control and lead the Hebrews in this uncertain period, God gave him the Ten Commandments as a moral and spiritual guide. Because of the negative, rebellious attitude of the Hebrews during this period, and because of their primitive understanding of the moral and spiritual laws, it was necessary to phrase the Ten Commandments in terms of "Thou shalt not."

From the Ten Commandments, you can learn specific "prosperity and success teachings" that can cause you to depart from limited living. They can help you to experience liberation from less than the best in your life. To succeed means "to obtain favorable results." The Ten Commandments show you how to do just that.

The first four Commandments have to do with man's right attitude toward God as a rich and loving Father, and his right relationship with God—both with man's indwelling God-nature and with the universal God.

The last six Commandments have to do with man's right attitudes toward, and right relationship with, his fellowman.

All of the Ten Commandments contain powerful teachings in prosperous living that you need to understand and apply—especially when, like the rebellious Hebrews, you are tempted to compromise and settle for less than the best life during your wilderness periods. As you use them, they can become your "prosperity and success commandments" too!

THE FIRST PROSPERITY COMMANDMENT

1. "THOU SHALT LOOK ONLY TO GOD AS THE SOURCE OF THY GUIDANCE AND ABUNDANT SUPPLY."

"Thou shalt have no other gods before me."

(Exodus 20:3)

The Egyptians had many gods. It was confusing to the Hebrews. Moses tried to teach them to look only to the One

God for their guidance and supply. They were forced to do this in the wilderness when they were provided with manna for only one day at a time. In this way, a loving Father was forcing them to learn the first prosperity commandment—to look only to Him for their guidance and abundance.

When you take up the power of thought and begin to use the inner laws of the mind to manifest your outer supply, the same thing may happen to you. *If you have been looking to outside circumstances for guidance and supply, there comes a time when there is no outside source to look to!* You may be forced to turn *within* to seek God's innate wisdom in order to be guided to your immediate supply. To do this is to learn the greatest prosperity secret of all.

HOW A SCHOOLTEACHER BECAME WEALTHY

A schoolteacher began affirming God as the source of her supply at a time when her life was filled with financial limitation. Her daily prayer was: *"I promptly and lovingly thank the Father for each of His gifts to me today. I am putting my trust in God for my supply. I am not depending upon persons or conditions. Thou, O God, art my mighty resource."*

Gradually her success began to unfold until she had become financially independent. She prospered in her profession. She inherited unexpected gifts of money, property, and jewelry. Her financial assets grew to include stocks, a comfortable home, and a nice car. Later she said, "Thanks to my recognition of God as my Almighty Resource, I have become a wealthy woman."

She proved that when you trust God as the source of your supply and when you decree that He is guiding you in claiming it, the rich substance of the universe (which has been called "the body of God") goes to work for you in countless ways to multiply your abundance and to make it permanent.

THE SECOND PROSPERITY COMMANDMENT

2. "THOU SHALT HOLD NO MENTAL IMAGE OF FINANCIAL
   LACK, OF LIMITED LIVING, OR OF FAILURE."

"Thou shalt not make unto thee a graven image."
(Exodus 20:4)

A "graven image" symbolizes hard, fixed attitudes which produce hard, fixed results of disease, financial lack, inharmony, confusion, and failure. This type of thinking is often brought to your attention by the words of others. The important thing is not to accept those limited thoughts and words, or hold to them.

When mental images of lack, limitation, or failure try to get your attention, say to them mentally and verbally: *"No, I do not accept this as the Prosperous Truth about this situation, or about me and my life."* Deny any appearance with the thought, *"No, No, No."* *Many a health problem has been cured when someone mentally said, "No," while people around them were talking of ills.*

Decree for any type of limitation: *"There is no absence of life, substance or intelligence anywhere, so there is no absence of life, substance or intelligence in this situation now."*

The mind is stimulated by bold ideas of health, wealth and happiness. *When you cannot demonstrate in a small way, you can demonstrate in a big way!* If you have been aiming for something that has not come into your life, deliberately expand your mental image and *aim for something bigger.* Declare: *"This or something better. Let my unlimited abundance appear now."*

There is an old saying, *"The highest is the nearest."* The rich substance of the universe always wants to flow forth in an unlimited way rather than in a small way. As you deliberately reverse your mental images from lack and failure to bold new images of abundant success, good things can then begin to happen to you.

HOW A FAMOUS GOLFER SUCCEEDED

A famous golfer discovered that the secret of his success was in the mental images he deliberately pictured about his golf game. He found that a certain type of swing wasn't enough to make him a winner. Strategy and attitudes were often more effective than his swing. When asked the secret of his fantastic success as a golfer, he said it was mentally picturing each step of his game ahead of time.

In his early years on the golf course, this man did not do this and he was a failure. His rise as a professional golfer came quickly after he learned to deliberately picture success for his game rather than expecting failure.

Good results increase when you mentally picture them first. Begin to get free of graven, fixed images of financial lack by declaring often: *"I will hold no mental pictures of financial lack, of limited living, or of failure. My abundant good cannot be limited now."*

THE THIRD PROSPERITY COMMANDMENT

3. "THOU SHALT NOT SPEAK WORDS OF FAILURE, POVERTY, UNHAPPINESS, OR DISEASE."

"Thou shalt not take the Name of Jehovah thy God in vain."

(Exodus 20:7)

Here is a little known prosperity secret that Moses tried to point out to the Hebrews centuries ago! *Your concept of the nature of God makes you what you are.* It affects your health, your appearance, your home, your business. It affects the kind of friends (and enemies) you have. It affects the kind of people you meet. *Of all the important things in your life, the one that matters most is your idea of God, because that determines everything else.*

The name and nature of God is Good. When you speak words of Good, you are speaking of God, His nature and His universe of lavish abundance in the highest form. Conversely when you speak words of failure, poverty, unhappiness or disease, you are cursing God's nature and taking His Name in vain. When you refuse to speak such negative words, you then have the power to dissolve such negative conditions. *Your words are creative — they are God-in-action.*

Jehovah emphasized the power of speaking His Name in positive ways when He showed Moses how to get the Israelites out of Egyptian bondage. He instructed Moses to say to Pharaoh, *"I AM* hath sent me." (Exodus 3:14)

HOW HE BECAME A FAMOUS PLAYWRIGHT

When a young man was working as a bellhop in a southern California hotel, he conceived the idea of writing a play. He had gained knowledge of the success power that can be released in affirming the words, *"I AM."* He began to say daily in his prayers, *"I am a successful playwright. I am, I am, I am."*

It seemed a preposterous idea for this hardworking bellhop, who had no training in writing or theater work. He decided to do the logical thing and write his play about a familiar subject—a bellhop in a hotel. His play was later produced with the help of Al Jolson and was a success on Broadway. He continued to use *"I AM"* statements and became a successful metaphysical lecturer and teacher, traveling throughout the United States and abroad.

THE FOURTH PROSPERITY COMMANDMENT

4. "THOU SHALT LET GO AND LET GOD WORK FOR YOUR WHOLE GOOD OF HEALTH, WEALTH AND HAPPINESS."

"Remember the Sabbath Day to keep it holy."

(Exodus 20:8)

Under the Jewish law, no one was allowed to work on the seventh day or Sabbath. After having worked for six days, they believed one should relax and give the fruits of his labor time to show forth results. This same success principle applies on the mental and spiritual levels of life.

The Sabbath symbolizes a time of cessation of effort. After you have used the first three prosperity commandments, you can see the wisdom of doing this:

First. You look to God for guidance and abundant supply.

Second. You hold no mental images of financial lack or failure. You firmly picture abundant supply and success.

Third. You speak no words of failure, poverty, unhappiness or disease. Instead you speak words of health, prosperity, well-being and divine order constantly. After doing these things, you reach a point where you are ready to let go and let God's abundant goodness work in, through, and for your health, wealth and happiness.

To accomplish anything worthwhile, you need a Sabbath. *If you do not let a thing alone when you have done all you can about it, it cannot grow.* The fishermen have a valuable saying: "There is a time to fish and there is a time to dry the nets."

There is a time for work and there is a time for rest. *Many people miss their intended prosperity and success because they are constantly trying so hard that they never observe a Sabbath.* They need to rest from their labors so their good can come to fruition. *This is a prosperity secret that cannot be by-passed if you wish to experience successful results in your life.*

When you have done all you know to do in inner and outer ways to either solve an old problem or to create some new good in your life and the results have not come, *you need to cease trying!* Give yourself this mental treatment: *"I let go and let God work for my whole good of health, wealth and happiness now. Having done all that I know to do about this situation, I now rest, relax, let go. I stand firm in the goodness of God. The finished results now come forth in this situation quickly and in peace. I give thanks and rejoice as those results appear in my life now."*

You can always tell when you are ready to observe such periods of letting go. When you have done all you know to do about a situation, you will begin to think less and less about it. Your mind will seek peace and rest from the subject. You have already mentally released it to work out in the best way. As you turn your attention to other things, your desired good will come!

THE FIFTH PROSPERITY COMMANDMENT

5. "THOU SHALT USE HONORABLY GOD'S LOVE AND WISDOM IN ALL PHASES OF THY LIFE."

"Honor thy father and thy mother."

(Exodus 20:12)

This is a literal command to esteem your earthly parents, who are responsible for your physical existence, and who provided your necessities early in life. Right adjustment in human relations begins with proper respect for the first people you knew, your parents or those representing them in your life. *"I am in true relationship with all people and with all situations now,"* is an excellent statement to bring about happiness in such relationships.

There is also a metaphysical meaning to this commandment: The wisdom teachings of the past have all emphasized the law of polarity as a necessity for successful living The law of polarity taught that you must use both wisdom and love in order to succeed in life. These qualities are often symbolized in the Bible by the masculine and feminine genders.

In reviewing the experiences in your life in which you feel you failed, you will find that one of these qualities was missing! You either used wisdom or love, but did not balance one with the other. You got an unbalanced result which you probably regarded as failure. *Success along all lines proceeds from a balanced use of love and wisdom.*

It is wise to begin a new day or a new project with this thought: *"Infinite wisdom guides me, divine love prospers me, and I am successful in everything I do. Love and wisdom are now united in me."*

A wise way to balance love and wisdom is this: No matter how much evil tries to appear in your world, refuse to speak of it. The mystics have long taught that evil appearances are undeveloped good. As you refuse to speak of evil and bless troublesome situations with love and wisdom, the good develops.

HOW A MOTHER HELPED HER TROUBLED TEENAGE DAUGHTER

A teenager quit school, was fired from several jobs, got into questionable association with others, and began keeping late hours. Trying to talk to her did not help. Neither did punishment or harsh discipline. Various family counseling groups failed to reach her.

Her mother refused to discuss her child's negative behavior with anyone. Often she prayerfully affirmed for her daughter: *"All is well. God reigns in you and in your life. Divine love and wisdom are at work. You are God's child and He loves you. Only abundant good and abundant growth shall come from this experience."*

To others this seemed a foolish course of action, but the mother persisted. She knew that people changed in unexpected moments. What we are tempted to look upon in scorn may be the Higher Self being born in another's experience.

Gradually her daughter began to respond. She spent more time at home. She was more truthful and dependable. She obtained a job and kept it. She became active in her church. She finally returned to school and became an honor student.

What a different result might have come forth had her mother not known how to call on divine love and wisdom, and declare their activity in this experience!

THE SIXTH PROSPERITY COMMANDMENT

6. "THOU SHALT NOT KILL THY ABUNDANT GOOD BY BE-
LIEVING IN LESS THAN THY ABUNDANT GOOD."

"Thou shalt not kill."

(Exodus 20:13)

When you are careful not to destroy another's courage
and faith, you are obeying this prosperity commandment.
Man has no right to deprive anyone of life for he cannot
replace life. When man deprives another of courage and
he may be said to "kill" him.

HOW AN ACCOUNTANT HELPED EVERYONE
IN HIS OFFICE

An accountant was working in an office with a group
of people who were dissatisfied with their jobs. It was dis-
couraging to listen to all the criticism and dissatisfaction
that was expressed there every day. This accountant realized that these people were killing their good with all their
negative words.

This employee began arriving at the office half an hour
early every morning. He would write down the name of
each employee and declare for him: *"There is good for
you. You ought to have it, so you claim it now. Your good
is at hand and quickly appears for you now."* During the
day when fellow workers spoke in terms of dissatisfaction,

he repeated the thought: *"Your good is at hand and quickly appears for you now."*

Happy things quickly happened. One man decided to retire and move out of town to his ranch. Another received a job offer with a leading law firm. It included a promotion and pay increase. Several others passed tests for better jobs with their company. One finally passed the required tests and received a certified public accountant's license, after having wanted it for ten years! The entire group was blessed after only one of them held to the thought, *"Your good it at hand."*

Always your good is at hand. How often you may have destroyed it through your idle thoughts and words of dissatisfaction. How quickly you can recoup when you change your words.

THE SEVENTH PROSPERITY COMMANDMENT

7. "THOU SHALT NOT ADULTERATE THY GOOD."

"Thou shalt not commit adultery."

(Exodus 20:14)

The word "adultery" comes from the same root as the word "adulterate." It means to corrupt or make impure by the admixture of a baser substance. This commandment has to do with moral living and with clean thinking.

To adulterate mentally means to mix the thought of good with the thought of limitation. The allegorical Adam and Eve were instructed in this success principle when they were told not to eat of the tree of the knowledge of good and evil.

Everytime you think of good, then mix it up with the belief in limitation, you are mentally committing adultery. When you compromise and settle for less than the best in life, you are adulterating your good by mixing it up with a belief in the necessity for accepting a limited way of life as a permanent arrangement.

To settle for ill health, financial difficulties, inharmony, or confusion is to adulterate one's blessings. This causes one to receive a mixed result in his life. When you are tempted to settle for less than the best in life declare: *"I have a divine right to the best. I now trust my divine rights to bring me out right in experiencing the best. I do not believe in mixture. I do not believe in failure. I believe in complete success. I do not accept mixture. I do not accept failure. I accept only complete success."*

A BUSINESSMAN GOT A CAR BUT WITH STRINGS ATTACHED AND LEARNED A VALUABLE LESSON

A businessman from the State of Virginia recently shared with me this experience in which he felt he had adulterated his good in a financial transaction, but learned a lesson in the process:

"I would like to share with you a recent prosperity demonstration which points up a lesson stressed in your prosperity books—a lesson my wife and I had forgotten until recently.

"Our old car was beginning to give some trouble, so we were forced to consider getting another car. Because it had been so long since we had purchased a car, we were shocked to find out how much they now cost. As we kept working to think prosperously, we finally accepted the idea that we could have a brand new car, not just a newer used car.

"Then I wrote out a prosperity statement concerning what we wanted and gave thanks that the money to pay for it was being provided. After doing this, we rapidly made a very favorable trade. The money to pay for it was provided by my brother-in-law's bank with payments to match.

"It was only much later that it dawned on me that I had limited the deal. I should have specified in my thinking, list-making and in my prosperity statements that the money would manifest with no strings attached.

"Nevertheless, I have learned a valuable lesson from the experience: *First*, that I can get results from the simple technique I used. *Second*, that I should have been more specific in my desires concerning the financial results I wished to obtain. The good that came from this apparent oversight was that I will be more careful and specific in my words from now on. Thought you would enjoy this demonstration twist."

Do not adulterate your good by speaking a half-truth. Claim your whole good with bold thoughts and words that describe what you actually want.

THE EIGHTH PROSPERITY COMMANDMENT

8. "THOU SHALT NOT TRY TO GET SOMETHING FOR NOTHING."

"Thou shalt not steal."

(Exodus 20:15)

Emerson wrote of this prosperity commandment when he said that for everything there is a price and if the price is not paid, not that thing but something else is obtained. "It is impossible for a man to be cheated by anyone but himself," he declared in his essay on *Compensation*.[1]

When you try to get something for nothing, you only cheat yourself. *One reason there is poverty in the midst of this abundant universe is because there are still people in the world who think they can get something for nothing.* When they attempt it, they make no contact with universal substance or with the substance of rich ideas within themselves. So they remain in a state of lack.

When you are tempted to try to get something for nothing, remind yourself that you are only delaying your good. It must first be earned in the consciousness of your own thoughts and feelings before there can be any permanent outer result.

HOW A CHRONIC ILLNESS WAS FINALLY HEALED

A woman had a chronic health problem which the finest in medical treatment had been unable to cure. Finally she learned that lasting health could come only by developing a health consciousness. She stopped talking about her health in negative terms. She began to read books on healing. She took physical exercise, tried a new diet prescribed by her physician, and began leading a more balanced life of work,

1. From *The Writings of Ralph Waldo Emerson* (New York, N.Y.: Random House, Inc., 1940).

play and rest. She worked daily in her flower garden, enjoyed sun baths, and took long walks in the fresh air.

She made a Wheel of Fortune for health on which she placed pictures of the active, healthy life she desired to lead. As she viewed this map daily she declared: *"I am the radiant child of God. My mind, body and affairs now reflect His radiant perfection."* She began to praise her body and her world. She began to praise other people. She made it a point to associate with people who talked about health. She terminated membership in one organization whose members spent most of their meeting periods discussing their health problems.

She planned ahead for special events which she began looking forward to: plays, movies, concerts, art exhibits, dinner parties. This helped her to picture herself as active, healthy, and able to attend those planned events. She constantly blessed her body with increased energy, and her life with increased activity. She gave thanks that she was whole and well.

As she worked in these ways to develop a consciousness of increased health, she was able to replace previous beliefs in the necessity of fatigue, ill health, old age, inactivity. Her new consciousness began to take control of her thoughts, her feelings, and of her body. Her life began to reflect the beautiful pictures of health and happiness that she had placed on her Wheel of Fortune for health.

You cannot steal your good. It will come automatically when you adjust your thinking to receive it. For this purpose you will enjoy declaring often these words: *"I do not try to get something for nothing. I am now developing a*

consciousness of peace, health and plenty. As I do so, those
results come to me."

THE NINTH PROSPERITY COMMANDMENT

9. "THOU SHALT NOT BEAR FALSE WITNESS AGAINST GOD,
THE SOURCE OF ALL THE GOOD IN THYSELF, IN THY
NEIGHBORS, OR IN THY WORLD."

"Thou shalt not bear false witness against thy neighbor."

(Exodus 20:16)

The word "neighbor" means those with whom you are in
close association. Your closest neighbor is your own indwelling God-nature. Your next closest neighbor is the Divine nature in your family, friends, and business associates.
There is also a universal Divine nature for good in all people and in all situations. It is only waiting to be recognized
and released in order to produce happy results in one's life
and in the world.

You bear false witness against your neighbor every time
you listen to gossip and negative talk about him. You bear
false witness when you state that he is ill and then discuss
his symptoms, or when you state that he is unsuccessful and
is having a hard time financially. To state these things is
to view him from a human standpoint only. However, he is
also a spiritual being containing divine potentialities far be-
yond your wildest dreams. You can help release his Divine

nature by declaring for him: *"I no longer bear false witness against you. I behold you as you truly are—an all-conquering son of God."*

You bear false witness against yourself when you say, "I cannot afford this" or "I just cannot make it financially." This may seem true from a human standpoint. But problems can only be solved from a divine standpoint. *The divinity within you is never poor!* Your God-self is rich. It will always show you the way to increased success if you ask to be shown, and then dare to follow the guidance that comes. Remind yourself often: *"God makes no mistakes and produces no failures. I am a complete success because God made me."*

HOW YOU CAN KEEP THIS PROSPERITY COMMANDMENT

You can keep this prosperity commandment by declaring: *"I never talk financial lack or limitation. I speak words of abundance. I bear witness to my heritage of abundance. I express the prospering power of Universal Intelligence in wisdom, love and good judgment in handling all my financial affairs now."*

You bear false witness against the universal God if you fail to recognize Him as the source of your supply, and if you fail to put Him first financially. *When people have financial problems, they are not recognizing God as the source of their supply. They are not putting Him first fi-*

*nancially through consistent giving of their tithes to His
work.*

The law is exact. *When you withhold from God, your
good is withheld from you in some form.* God has given you
all that you have and all that you can hope to have as
health, wealth and happiness. One-tenth of your blessings
is a small amount to return to Him in appreciation. To do
so keeps the abundance of the universe flowing to you in
ever-increasing ways. "You'll never find a tither in the poor-
house," is an old and true saying.

Affirm often: *"I do not bear false witness against God,
the Giver of all Good, by withholding my tithes. I give
richly, joyously, freely of my tithes to God's work. I bear
witness to the truth that God is the source of my supply. I
joyously put God first financially and my life is orderly,
harmonious and abundantly blessed."*

THE TENTH PROSPERITY COMMANDMENT

10. "THOU SHALT CLAIM THINE OWN GOOD!"

"Thou shalt not covet."

(Exodus 20:17)

*You never need the good another has. It would not satis-
fy you, if you had it. If you covet another's good as your
own, you are asking for trouble. What belongs to another is
not yours by divine right. If it were, it would have come to
you in the first place. Since it is not yours by divine right,
it would do you no good even if you got it.*

HOW TO CLAIM YOUR GOOD INSTEAD OF COVETING SOMEONE ELSE'S GOOD

A woman coveted another's husband as her own. She got him but he was not what she had expected. Later she met and fell in love with someone who was free to marry her and would have, but she had taken another's husband and was not free. Through coveting what belonged to someone else, she came to grief and disappointment, as did several other people involved in this questionable relationship.

What belongs to another never quite fits your needs and would not satisfy you. There is no need to covet what another has, or mentally try to force it to you. *Realize that another's good is an indication that similar good is on its way to you.* Help bring it forth by declaring: *"I am in contact with the source of that good. The divine equivalent of that good is on its way to me now. I gratefully accept it."*

SUMMARY

1. Moses has often been described as the emancipator of his people from Egyptian bondage. He was that, but much more. His mission was also a prosperity mission, to help the Hebrews realize they did not have to depend upon the Egyptians for their prosperity, that God was the source of their supply, and could lead them into far more in their own long-awaited Promised Land. When you realize this, you can see why the Ten Commandments are powerful "prosperity commandments."

2. From the Ten Commandments, you can learn specific "prosperity and success teachings" that can cause you to depart from limited living. They can help you to experience liberation from less than the best in your life. To succeed means "to obtain favorable results." The Ten Commandments show you how to do just that.

3. The first four Commandments have to do with man's right attitude toward God as a rich and loving Father, and his right relationship with God—both with man's indwelling God-nature and with the universal God. The last six Commandments have to do with man's right attitudes toward, and right relationship with, his fellow-man.

4. All of the Ten Commandments contain powerful teachings in prosperous living that you need to understand and apply, especially when, like the rebellious Hebrews, you are tempted to compromise and settle for less than the best in life during your wilderness periods.

5. Here are the Prosperity Commandments:

a) "THOU SHALT LOOK ONLY TO GOD AS THE SOURCE OF THY GUIDANCE AND SUPPLY."

b) "THOU SHALT HOLD NO MENTAL IMAGE OF FINANCIAL LACK, OF LIMITED LIVING, OR OF FAILURE."

c) "THOU SHALT NOT SPEAK WORDS OF FAILURE, POVERTY, UNHAPPINESS, OR DISEASE."

d) "THOU SHALT LET GO AND LET GOD WORK FOR YOUR WHOLE GOOD OF HEALTH, WEALTH AND HAPPINESS."

e) "THOU SHALT USE HONORABLY GOD'S LOVE AND WISDOM IN ALL PHASES OF THY LIFE."

f) "THOU SHALT NOT KILL THY ABUNDANT GOOD BY BELIEVING IN LESS THAN THY ABUNDANT GOOD."

g) "THOU SHALT NOT ADULTERATE THY GOOD."

h) "THOU SHALT NOT TRY TO GET SOMETHING FOR NOTHING."

i) "THOU SHALT NOT BEAR FALSE WITNESS AGAINST GOD, THE SOURCE OF ALL THE GOOD IN THYSELF, IN THY NEIGHBORS, OR IN THY WORLD."

j) "THOU SHALT CLAIM THINE OWN GOOD."

THE PROSPERITY LAW
OF OPULENCE

— Chapter 7 —

You came into this world divinely supplied. You brought your wealth with you in the form of talents and mind powers. You should have no financial problems. You should be rich in mind and in outward manifestation. Poverty is a form of hell caused by man's blindness to God's unlimited good for him.

The word "opulence" means "wealth, riches, abundance." As the rich child of a loving Father, created in His image, you should be living opulently in this lavish universe that has been provided for you!

As you awaken to this prosperous Truth about yourself and about the universe, you will find your soul longing for the opulence that is your heritage. Do not suppress your longing for it. Do not ignorantly say that you are becoming "materially minded."

The more you study the prosperous Truth about yourself and about the universe, the more sensitive you will become to beauty and opulence. The more your soul will long for it

142

in your life. The more your soul will feed on the wealth and beauty of the universe. Increased abundance will give you a sense of peace and satisfaction that nothing else can.

The Bible's great leaders lived opulently. Many of them became millionaires as they used the same laws of opulence that are available to you and to me. *Although his followers criticized Moses about many things during their wilderness wanderings, they never criticized him for teaching them how to prosper!*

Moses had learned the prosperity law of opulence when he was a prince at the court of Pharaoh. This knowledge, coupled with faith in God as the source of his supply, enabled Moses to provide for his followers over a forty-year period in the wilderness. He did it in both mystical and practical ways.

The wearing of old and mended clothes is very common in the East, even today. When traveling there, one can see thousands of men, women and children in rags. However, the rich seldom wear old clothes. The Hebrews were supplied so abundantly during their wilderness wanderings that they did not have to wear old clothes. Nor were they without shoes. Their large flocks supplied them with an abundance of wool and leather which they used for garments and shoes.

Even today when a man in the East has good clothes and shoes, he is considered very well-to-do. When they are not well-dressed, the people of the East are not welcomed at many public and social events. *The Hebrews lacked nothing during their wilderness sojourn. They were considered "well-to-do."* A rich Father provided for all their needs.

They were later reminded: "These forty years the Lord thy God hath been with thee; thou hast lacked nothing." (Deuteronomy 2:7)

WHY OPULENCE IS NECESSARY TO YOU

Opulence is a necessity to your inner and outer success. Jehovah pointed this out through the instructions He gave in the Book of Exodus for building and lavishly furnishing the Hebrews' tabernacle. Even though it was a portable place of worship, which was to be moved about in the wilderness, the tabernacle was to be constructed of the finest materials including acacia wood, goats' hair, and rams' skins. It was to be furnished with linens, silver and gold.

Jehovah pointed out the necessity of opulence through the specific instructions given for the clothes that were to be created for the High Priest. His garments were to be made of fine linens in brilliant colors. They were to be set in gold, adorned with emeralds, diamonds and other precious stones. Described as "garments of glory" they were to be made by "skilled workmen" equivalent to our modern designers. They were to be worn for "glory and beauty." (Exodus 28:2)

As the rich child of a loving Father, you are also a "priest of God." *You are entitled to wear and enjoy those things which enrich your soul and enhance your world.* This is an important way to get out of bondage to lack. Developing a prosperous consciousness begins from "the skin out."

Probably none of us would care to wear the ornate robes that Aaron wore as the first High Priest of Israel. Yet we are entitled to all the riches of God, both in our interior and exterior worlds—all that we can mentally accept and wisely use.

It is significant that Jehovah gave instructions for building and lavishly furnishing the tabernacle while the Hebrews were still in the wilderness. It is significant that Aaron was instructed to wear elegant garments in that barren place.

Why?

Because right there in that barren wilderness, the Hebrews needed to lift their vision to opulence. Developing an "opulence consciousness" later helped them to get out of that wilderness. Also they needed to lift their vision to opulence in order to receive and accept the unlimited abundance that awaited them in their Promised Land—a wealth that was to multiply many, many times over the years.

HOW TO EXPAND YOUR OPULENCE CONSCIOUSNESS

This is the secret of opulence: Begin now in your present circumstances to get ready for the good you want. Do what you can to prepare your consciousness to mentally accept more. *You have to make the desert-like places in your life as beautiful, rich and harmonious as possible if you want to increase your good.*

Do not sit down and wait for the blessings you want to come to you. *Do the most you can with what you have if*

you want to receive more. Realtors know that the quickest
way to sell a house is by fixing it up. *Fix up your wilderness!*

Use what you already have. The Hebrews had gold,
silver, jewels and other finery they had brought from Egypt.
They had gained much of this portable wealth through an
exchange of assets with the Egyptians at the last minute
before departing from Egypt, where they had been forced
to leave behind household supplies, lands and crops.

Not to have used some of the vast portable wealth they
had brought with them from Egypt would have violated
"the law of use." Do not store up your finest possessions,
waiting for special occasions for their use. Use them now.
This practice not only makes you feel rich, but it opens
the way for more abundance to come to you.

THE SURPRISE INHERITANCE

There once was a man with two sons. When he passed
on, this father left a farm to each of his two sons. The
eldest son received the home place, which was prosperous
because it was situated in a fertile valley.

The other son received a farm in a distant state. When
he inspected his inheritance, this son was disappointed. His
farm consisted of several hundred acres of wasteland with
a shack and some outbuildings on it. They were all badly
in need of repair. There was not even a well for water.

Bitter over his inheritance, this son thought, "What could
I raise on this rocky, waterless waste land?"

He returned home to his rented farm and for several years
struggled, barely making a living. He brooded bitterly over

the great injustice of his father's will. His brother was prospering from the farm he had inherited.

While listening to the radio one day, the second son heard the speaker say, "Live today. Begin now doing the thing you want to do. Begin now being the person you want to be. Begin now with what you have. Your opportunity lies within yourself. God will help you when once you have made the start."

These words haunted the listener, *"Begin now with what you have. God will help you when once you have made the start."* He decided he must do the best he could with what he had if he wanted to receive more. He stopped criticizing his barren farm. He decided to appreciate it and fix it up. He settled on that farm in the distant state and began working it.

The first thing he did was to hire a man to help drill for water. After many days of backbreaking work, there was no sign of water. When discouragement tried to set in he remembered the words, "God will help you when once you have made the start." He persevered.

After a day of deep drilling for water with no results, this man went to bed more depressed than ever. The next morning his small son awakened him, "Daddy, come quick! Black water is coming out of the well." That "black water" was oil. This man had become an instant millionaire.

In a few days he received a note from his father's attorney which enclosed a letter from his late father. It read:

"When you receive this message you will have discovered the treasure hidden in your land. Years ago I

learned there was oil on this property. I never told anyone because I wanted you to find it. I am aware that
you and your family have suffered hardships in moving onto this place, but I am sure you agree that the
reward you have found is more than worth the sacrifice you made. This is your land. Develop it, enjoy it
and you will prosper."

A postscript read:

"You won't need to dig for water anymore. You will
find a well under the mound of rocks in the yard. I
covered it so you would have to dig a well and discover
the oil."

DO'S AND DON'TS OF OPULENT THINKING

When you talk hard times you are sowing hard-times
seed, and by the sure law of growth, *that* is the kind of
harvest you will reap. Do not say money is scarce. The
very statement will scare it away from you. Never say that
times are hard with you. Such words will tighten your purse
strings so that money cannot get into it.

Deliberately think plenty, talk plenty and give thanks for
plenty for yourself and for others. Never condemn anything in your home. If you want new furniture or clothing
to take the place of what you have, do not say that what
you have is old or shabby. Watch your words. See that you
talk like the child of a King. Picture yourself and your home
as you would like it to be. Bless what you have. Appreciate
it. Fix it up. Your actions will multiply your good.

HOW SHE GOT HER HUSBAND BACK

The law of opulence works on all levels of life, including that of human relationships.

A woman's husband became interested in someone else. When she realized it, this wife felt as though she was in a wilderness. She brooded over the situation until she realized that she must live as normally as possible if she wished to correct an abnormal situation. The day her husband asked for a divorce, he expected a scene. Instead his wife said, "Divorce is so final. Let us be sure. I will give you a divorce in three months if you still want it then." Relieved, he agreed.

This woman decided to make the best—instead of the worst—of this situation. She fixed up her wilderness by putting more effort into her homemaking. She tried to make things as beautiful and as pleasant as possible. She took more pains with her cooking and with her personal appearance.

As though nothing were wrong, she became active in her book club again. She took up several sports including golf and tennis. She ceased questioning her husband's coming and goings.

When she did the best she could with abnormal circumstances, they improved. Her husband ceased being away so much. Their life together resumed a more normal pattern. He began coming home for dinner again every night and quietly reading before the fire afterwards.

One morning three months later she said, "It is about time we made a decision about the divorce." Blankly he asked, "Who wants a divorce?" That settled it.

HOW SHE WAS HEALED OF ARTHRITIS

The law of opulence can be applied to one's health. A lady who suffered from arthritis kept thinking that *when* her health was better she would work in her flower garden again. She had also vowed to get back to her professional writing when she felt like it. As long as she kept waiting, no improvement came. She felt worse, weeds sprung up in her garden, and her writing ideas haunted her.

Finally she realized that it would be necessary to make the best of her present health if she wanted it to improve. She stopped criticizing her health. She stopped talking about "my arthritis." She went out into the flower garden and began boldly pulling weeds, even though it was physically painful.

Later she went into her study and worked on an article about gardening. Then she headed for the kitchen and made her husband's favorite pie, though she did not feel much like it. She reasoned that she could not just sit down and wait to be healed. She had tried that and it had not worked. She felt God would help her now that she had made a start toward normal living again.

As she purposely worked in her flower garden daily, she began to feel better. Gradually the pain subsided. Her writing and housework took on a normal perspective. Finally she was leading a normal, productive life again. But nothing had improved until she made a start toward it.

It pays to fix up the barren spots in your life. Live as normally as possible when faced with abnormal conditions. Do the best you can with what you have. This opens the way to opulence.

To help you make a start declare often: *"I begin now to talk plenty, think plenty, and give thanks for plenty. I use what I have with wisdom. I make the best of my present situation. God will help me as I make a start. Opulence is my divine right and I claim it in every phase of my world. I dare to 'fix up' my wilderness now."*

HOW YOUR GOOD CAN ARRIVE TEN TIMES QUICKER

Moses pointed out the tithing law of opulence to the Hebrews while they were still in the wilderness, and they never questioned his instructions—which had been given him by Jehovah right out of the ethers. As they tithed, they prospered accordingly. (Moses had earlier learned the universal practice of tithing in the temples of Egypt.)

The Hebrews were instructed to give *"all* of the tithe" of the land, seed, fruit, grain, wine, oil, the firstlings of the flock. "Whatever passeth under the rod, the tenth shall be holy unto Jehovah." (Leviticus 27:30-32; Deuteronomy 14:22, 23) He also reminded them that when they later entered their abundant Promised Land, the way to remain prosperous would be by continuing to tithe. They were instructed not to take their blessings for granted once they had obtained them. (Deuteronomy 12:10-12)

People may be prospered without tithing but it is hard work. That is the trial and error method. The word "tithe" means "tenth." *Tithing brings success to you ten times easier and ten times quicker.* When you take God as your financial partner, you are bound to prosper. Psychologically and spiritually, you expect it.

The idea of material prosperity as the reward for faithfulness is common to the Old Testament. Moses commanded obedience to the inner and outer laws he laid down, assuring the Hebrews that every blessing would come to Israel: prosperity, health, protection and guidance. Should the Hebrews forget God as the giver of all, they would perish. If the Hebrews were faithful, there would be no poor. Loyalty to God would bring inevitable prosperity. All manner of bountifulness would be theirs. His promises have stood the test of time over the centuries. *Those who look to God for guidance and supply experience inevitable prosperity, and all manner of bountifulness.* Those who do not experience all manner of problems.

HOW TWO MEN BECAME MILLIONAIRES

A businessman was "down on his luck" when he met a religious worker who assured him that if he would tithe, he would prosper. Like the Hebrews of old, he never questioned the instruction but decided to try it. He gave that religious worker more than a tenth of his last dollar—15¢. He continued tithing and later struck oil. When asked the secret of his great fortune he said, "I couldn't miss. I was in partnership with God and He *made* geology!"

Various schemes have been worked out for getting rich quick. Most of them fail because they have no spiritual basis. They do not include God who is the source of all wealth. Tithing is as certain in its prospering power as is the law of gravity. Tithing is based upon universal prosperity principles that cannot fail.

Soon after the famous Texan, R. G. LeTourneau, started tithing he received an idea for a new type of road machinery. He used it and made a fortune. One of his engineers said, "We don't know where he gets all of his ideas, but most of them are not only good, they are new and revolutionary." *Million dollar ideas came to him after he began tithing.*

FROM POVERTY TO A $13 MILLION DOLLAR INCOME

There once was a man who decided to go to Florida to get in on a boom. The boom burst about the time he arrived and he was soon in bad shape financially. He heard it was possible to tithe one's way to opulence, and decided to find out.

The first year he tithed his income increased 60 percent. The next year his income increased 100 percent. He continued to tithe and became owner of one of the largest real estate companies in the state. One year recently he grossed more than $13 million dollars.

He taught the tithing law of opulence to one of his salesmen who was in debt. Within a year the salesman had paid off his indebtedness and had a sizeable bank account. Later he went into business for himself and became exceedingly prosperous.

HOW THEY WENT FROM RAGS TO RICHES

William Colgate went out into the world as a poor boy seeking his fortune. He found it after he started tithing. He became the owner of one of the largest soap companies in the world. The Heinz family started tithing and built a fortune in the pickle business. Mr. Kraft started tithing early in his business career. He founded the Kraft Cheese Company, and you know the opulent results.

A businessman of my acquaintance had always struggled financially. He started tithing at the age of 50, and quickly went from rags to riches. When asked the secret of his startling success so late in life he would always reply, "I tithed my way to prosperity, and anyone can do it."

A salesman not only saved his home from foreclosure after he started tithing, his marriage was saved, too. A widow, who had been alone for twenty years, happily remarried after she started tithing. One man even stopped drinking after his wife started tithing in secret.

Most people think that when they are prosperous, *then* they will begin to tithe. The law of opulence works the other way: *You become prosperous because you give first and consistently*. The law of opulence is "give and *then* you will receive. Don't expect to receive when you are not giving."

HOW TO INVOKE THE LAW OF OPULENCE THROUGH GIVING PROPERLY

The law of opulence includes *where* you give your tithe. You place your faith where you place your money. You should give your tithes at the point or points where you are receiving spiritual help and inspiration.

A businesswoman once wrote, "I do not understand it. I am using the laws of prosperity, yet I am not prospering. I have an apartment house that I cannot keep rented. Don't tell me to tithe. I am already doing so."

When asked, *"Where* are you tithing?" she replied, "I cannot see that it matters where I give. I tithe to the church that I used to attend because they still send me pledge cards. But I attend another church now where I find far more inspiration and practical help."

It was suggested that *where* she gave her tithes is as important as *how* she spent the other 90 percent of her income. She would not go to one doctor for help, yet pay another. She would not go to one restaurant to be fed, yet pay at another restaurant. Neither should she give at one point when she had received spiritual help elsewhere.

Where you give your tithes *is* very important. It may not be the largest spiritual organization or the most prominent. You should give to that individual in spiritual work, or to that organization, where you are receiving spiritual help and inspiration. The act of tithing provides you with sufficient funds to distribute in several ways if you wish. Such giving makes you feel rich, as well as enriching the recipient(s).

"Should not each spiritual organization and its workers demonstrate their own supply?" someone has asked. Certainly, but God supplies their needs through those whom they serve. God is their supply, but man is the channel of that supply. If you look to such a work or organization for your help and inspiration, it is natural that you become a channel through which God supplies that work or that organization's needs. It is a poor rule that does not work both ways.

You should deliberately prosper those who inspire and help you meet life's problems victoriously—if for no other reason than to safeguard your own best interest! You should make your chosen channel of inspiration as prosperous as possible, in order to keep it free from financial burdens and so that it may continue to minister spiritually, unhindered by material care.

WHY THE WORLD LOVES PROSPEROUS SPIRITUAL WORKERS

There is another reason for prospering inspirational organizations and those in spiritual work:

As in the time of Moses, even now the world wants and needs spiritual organizations and workers who can tell you how to be prosperous, and who, through their own lives, are demonstrating that they know these prosperity laws. *The world loves, respects and listens to those in spiritual work who have proved the laws of opulence. Such workers*

*have a high-powered consciousness that draws and inspires
a loyal following.* By giving to those in such a high-powered
consciousness, you tune in on that consciousness and open
the way to receive vast blessings of expanded good in your
own life.

WHY THE PRIESTS WERE MILLIONAIRES

Under the Mosaic law the priests of the Old Testament
were millionaires. The priestly tribe of Levi did not receive
any of the Promised Land later during the reign of Joshua.
Instead they received *all* of the tithes from the entire Promised Land:

> "For the Levites have no portion (of land) among
> you; for the priesthood of Jehovah is their inheritance."
>
> (Joshua 18:7)

> "Unto the children of Levi, I have given *all* the tithes
> in Israel for an inheritance."
>
> (Numbers 18:21)

In turn, the priests gave a tithe of the tithe known as "a
heave offering" to the tabernacle, temple or place of worship:

> "When ye take of the children of Israel the tithe
> which I have given you from them for your inheritance,
> then ye shall offer up a heave offering of it for Jehovah,
> a tithe of the tithe."
>
> (Numbers 18:26)

There are no short cuts in developing a prosperity consciousness of opulence. There are those who say, "I do not tithe to those who inspire me but I do show my appreciation with gifts." You would not take your doctor or lawyer a gift instead of paying him properly for his professional services. A spiritual consciousness is the result of a lifetime (or perhaps many lifetimes) of development. It's help is priceless to the one seeking it. Just appreciation opens the way for the expansion of your own consciousness of opulence.

There are people everywhere who are spiritually minded only up to their hip pockets. They give the Lord practically everything: Advice, excuses, good intentions, a little time and even a little energy—everything except the coin of the realm.

Not so of those who are developing a true opulence consciousness. It includes abundant generosity. *Sharing is always the beginning of opulent increase.*

HOW SHE RECEIVED $250

If you seem restricted from giving literally, you can always begin to tithe mentally first. Write out the name of the person, church or religious organization to whom you would like to be free to give a tithe. Then mentally give it.

A housewife had been helped by a spiritual counselor and wanted to show her appreciation, but no money was available. She thought, "I would like to give that person $25." Still nothing happened.

One day she decided to get definite. She wrote out, "I give thanks that $25 now comes to me to share with this person." That night at dinner she found a check for $250 beside her plate—a special gift from her husband. She quickly sent a tithe of $25 to the worker, as earlier planned.

HOW A RETIRED PERSON RECEIVED $100

A retired businesswoman was ill and asked the prayer assistance of a spiritual counselor. She asked, "Please come and pray with me in my home because I am unable to come to your office. I do not have a tithe offering to share in appreciation right now, but I will have one soon."

The counselor's prayers were the turning point. After months of lingering illness, recovery began for this woman following the counselor's visit. Soon this lady received a check for $100 from a friend. She sent a tithe of $10 from it to the counselor. When she had tithed *mentally*, the way had opened for her to literally receive and to share.

THEY HAD TO BE RESTRAINED FROM GIVING!

The Hebrews developed such an opulence consciousness in the wilderness that Moses had to finally restrain them from giving! The passage reads:

"The people were restrained from bringing, for the stuff they had was sufficient for all the work, and it was *too much*."

(Exodus 36:6, 7)

As you use the prosperity law of opulence in the various ways described in this chapter, you can get out of the wilderness of limitation into your Promised Land of lavish abundance. I trust the time will come when you will also have to be "restrained" from giving!

A happy ending from financial limitation can be a happy beginning in the Land of Opulence for you as you meditate often upon these rich words:

"I BEGIN RIGHT NOW TO THINK PLENTY, TALK PLENTY AND GIVE THANKS FOR PLENTY. I MAKE THE MOST OF MY PRESENT SITUATION. I BEGIN USING WHAT I HAVE. I TITHE MY WAY TO OPULENCE. GOD WILL HELP ME WHEN ONCE I MAKE THE START! MY SUCCESS COMES TEN TIMES EASIER AND TEN TIMES QUICKER AS I USE THE TITHING LAW OF OPULENCE. CONSISTENT SHARING IS ALWAYS THE BEGINNING OF MY CONSISTENTLY OPULENT INCREASE."

A SPECIAL NOTE FROM THE AUTHOR

"Through the generous outpouring of their tithes over the years, the readers of my books have helped me to financially establish three new churches—the most recent being a global ministry, the nondenominational *Unity Church Worldwide,* with headquarters in Palm Desert, California. Many thanks for your help in the past, and for all that you continue to share.

"You are also invited to share your tithes with the churches of your choice—especially those which teach the truths stressed in this book. Such churches would include the metaphysical churches of Unity, Religious Science, Divine Science, Science of Mind and other related churches, many of which are members of the International New Thought Movement. (For a list of such churches write The International New Thought Alliance, 7314 East Stetson Drive, Scottsdale, Arizona 85251.) Your support of such churches can help spread the prosperous Truth that mankind is now seeking in this New Age of metaphysical enlightenment."

SUMMARY

1. The word "opulence" means "wealth," "riches," "abundance." As the rich child of a loving Father, created in His image, you should be living opulently in this lavish universe that has been provided for you.

2. You came into this world divinely supplied. You brought your wealth with you in the form of talents and mind powers. You should have no financial problems. You should be rich in mind and in outward manifestation.

3. As you awaken to this properous Truth about yourself and about the universe, you will find your soul longing for the opulence that is your heritage. Do not suppress your longing for it.

4. The Bible's great leaders lived opulently. Although his followers criticized Moses about many things during their wilderness wanderings, they never critized him for teaching them how to prosper!

5. Moses had learned the prosperity law of opulence when he was a prince at the court of Pharaoh. This knowledge, coupled with faith in God as the source of his supply, enabled Moses to provide for his followers over a forty-year period in the wilderness. He did it in both mystical and practical ways.

6. The Hebrews lacked nothing during their wilderness sojourn. They were considered "well-to-do." Opulence is a necessity to your inner and outer success.

7. Jehovah pointed out the necessity of opulence through the specific instructions given for the clothes that were to be created for the High Priest, and through the erection of the lavish portable tabernacle in which the Hebrews worshipped during their wilderness sojourn. You too, are entitled to wear and enjoy those things which enrich your soul and enhance your world.

8. Right there in that barren wilderness, the Hebrews needed to lift their vision to one of abundance. Developing an "opulence consciousness" also helped them to get out of that wilderness.

9. You have to make the desert places in your life as beautiful, rich and harmonious as possible if you want to increase your good. So fix up your wilderness! Begin now with what you have. God will help you when once you have made the start. Never say that times are hard with you. Such words tighten your purse strings so that money cannot get into it. Think plenty, talk plenty and give thanks for plenty for yourself and for others. Live as normally as possible when faced with abnormal conditions. Your actions will multiply your good.

10. There are no short cuts in developing an opulence consciousness. Various schemes have been worked out for getting rich quick. Most of them fail because they have no spiritual basis. Tithing brings success to you ten times easier and ten times quicker. Sharing is always the beginning of opulent increase.

11. You can invoke the laws of opulence through tithing properly to that individual or organization through which you are receiving spiritual help and inspiration. You should deliberately prosper those who inspire and help you meet life's problems victoriously, not only to aid them financially, but also in order to safeguard your own best interest.

12. Under the Mosaic law, the priests of the Old Testament were millionaires. They were given none of the Promised Land, which could have been a burden for them to care for. Instead they were given *all* of the tithes of *all* of the Promised Land. This assured them freedom from material care or financial strain. As you use the prosperity law of opulence as described in this chapter, you can develop the opulence consciousness that the Hebrews began developing in the wilderness— a prosperity consciousness that was to prosper them for centuries to come!

THE MIRACLE LAW
OF PROSPERITY

— Chapter 8 —

The miracle law of prosperity is released through thanksgiving. Why? *Because the deliberate act of thanks liberates certain potent energies of mind and body that are not otherwise released. Through praise and thanksgiving, you can activate the dynamic powers of the subconscious and superconscious phases of your mind, which then act speedily in your behalf! It is possible through the deliberate act of thanksgiving to completely transform your life. Yes, thanksgiving is your miracle power for prosperity.*

The trick is to give thanks *first*—before there seems to be anything to give thanks for. When you give thanks anyway, your mental acceptance is accelerated. Your good is stepped up. It comes more quickly.

The Hebrews learned the miracle power of thanksgiving while still in the wilderness. Moses taught them to observe festival days not once or twice, but three times a year. (Exodus 23:14)

Their *first* annual festival was the Passover, commemorating their escape out of Egyptian bondage into freedom. Their *second* annual festival was called "the Feast of the Harvest" or "the Feast Day of the First Fruits." This consisted of one day set aside at the *beginning* of the harvest season. Their *third* annual festival was known as "the Feast of the Tabernacle." It was an ingathering at the close of the season, comparable to the day of Thanksgiving observed annually in the United States and Canada.

It is wise to set aside a day annually for recognizing your blessings, and that is easy enough to do at the close of the harvest season, or after you have obtained prosperous results in your life (symbolized by the Hebrews' *third* annual festival).

How much more often you would experience the miracle power of thanksgiving if, like the Hebrews, you would give thanks for the various problems you have already "passed over" (symbolized by their *first* annual festival).

You should also follow their example and praise and give thanks at the *beginning* of a new experience, rather than only after its completion (symbolized by their *second* annual festival).

Indeed, the miracle power of Thanksgiving is released by praising and giving thanks *before* there seems to be anything to praise and give thanks for! You should observe a "feast day of the first fruits" at the *beginning* of a new experience through which you expect to harvest your good. It can be the turning point from a mediocre way of life to one of lasting success.

HOW THANKSGIVING PUT FOOD ON THE TABLE AND PROVIDED QUICK CASH

You open the way for great demonstrations through the act of giving thanks *first* as you begin to work toward your goal.

A businesswoman had extra expenses. The payment of these expenses plus the payment of current bills was due. There was not nearly enough money to go around. She had affirmed and affirmed that there would be, but nothing had happened.

In desperation she thought, "What must I do? What prosperous thought must I think in order to meet this financial need?" Then she opened some inspirational literature and found these words: *"If substance does not increase for you, it is because you have been ungrateful and cynical."*

She thought, "That is true. I *have* been very ungrateful and cynical."

This reminded her of some notes she had taken at a lecture. They read:

"When your conditions are cold, still unyielding after you have been mentally treating them, you should go into a room by yourself and give thanks that Divine Substance does everything good for you now; that it supplies you, pays your debts and in every way blesses you. Speak to the gold in your affairs. Speak to your sick neighbor. Speak to your family problems. With a loud voice praise Divine Substance and call it forth as new life, new kindness, new bounty, new conditions."

These words had an electrifying effect. This woman realized how ungrateful and cynical she had become in tryings to solve her financial problems. She had criticized her bills. She had condemned her ability to pay them. She had criticized the unexpected experiences that had brought on the additional expenses. She had condemned her usual channels of income saying they were insufficient. *Her ingratitude had scared prosperity away from her.*

She went into a room alone and deliberately spoke words of praise and thanksgiving for the bills due, for the unpaid-for clothes hanging in her closet, for food she wished to see on the pantry shelves. Taking her wallet and checkbook in her hands, she gave thanks that they were filled to overflowing with Divine Substance. For an hour she remained in that room alone calling on Divine Substance, and giving thanks for its quick manifestation in her life as appropriate financial increase.

An hour later she received a long-distance call offering her special work which she was to do immediately. It paid her the equivalent of an extra month's pay. With it she met her financial obligations.

Many people have gone hungry down through the ages. Widespread famine has caused millions to starve. Why? History reveals that none of those starving civilizations observed the act of thanksgiving. The two most affluent countries in the world today are the United States and Canada. They are also the *only* two countries in the world that observe a national day of Thanksgiving annually! *There is prospering power in thanksgiving. People who give thanks do not starve. They prosper. So speak to the gold in your affairs. With a loud voice praise Divine Substance and call it forth as new life, new kindness, new bounty, and new conditions.*

HOW THANKSGIVING OPENED THE WAY TO PAY HIS BILLS

People sometimes neglect to give thanks for so long that things get very bad for them. Most of us have had hardships because we neglected to be thankful.

A businessman had learned the prospering power of giving thanks *first*. His bills were due and he was short on funds. Instead of condemning himself or his bills, he looked at them and said, "I give thanks for these bills. The people to whom they are owed think I am prosperous. Otherwise they would not have trusted me with credit. I give thanks for these bills because they are an indication of my ever-increasing prosperity now." He paid what he could, and he blessed the rest. Soon his "ever-increasing prosperity" had manifested and he paid the other bills.

You can invoke the miracle power of thanksgiving by giving thanks in the face of your problems, before there seems to be anything to be thankful for.

HOW A NURSE ACTIVATED HER PROSPERITY QUICKLY

A private nurse had finished an assignment but had not been paid. She was awaiting another assignment that had not come through. Her husband had been laid off from his job, and bills had accumulated.

One day when their creditors were pressing hard, this

woman became frightened. There was hardly enough food in the house for dinner that night. She visited a friend and recited their financial woes. The friend suggested that this nurse stop trying to figure out how things could work out financially, and that she start giving thanks that Divine Substance was already at work for her!

Together these friends declared: *"I give thanks that Divine Substance is at work for me now. I give thanks that the perfect results of Divine Substance now quickly appear in my financial affairs."* The nurse agreed to stop talking about her financial woes and to speak only in terms of appreciation for her blessings, both seen and unseen.

On the way home she thanked God over and over for His all-providing substance. She discovered there was enough food on the pantry shelf for dinner that night, though there would be no dessert. In a few minutes her husband arrived with the dessert—a quart of ice cream—which he had won!

The next morning's mail brought a check in payment of her completed nursing assignment. That same day she received a call to return to duty on a new case. Her husband's lay-off ended and he, too, returned to work. As she continued to give thanks *first*, her financial problems were all resolved.

THE "THANK YOU BOX" METHOD

The mother of a large family did not have ample supply with which to meet their needs. She took an old shoe box and converted it to a "thank you box."

She asked her children to write out the blessings they sought, and place them in the "thank you box." Once a week they would open the "thank you box" and go through their requests to see how many had been fulfilled.

These were farm people who needed rain for their crops. One week they were in the midst of a dry period. The mother wrote down these words which she put in the "thank you box": "Thank you God for rain—a regular downpour."

This happened on Tuesday. The next Sunday as they were going through their notes in the box, they realized that on Friday there had been "a regular downpour" of rain—the first in weeks!

On another occasion, her husband was having trouble with his car. He needed it in his work and also to make a special trip that had been planned. He had worked and worked on his car, trying to locate the mechanical trouble.

Finally his wife remembered the "thank you box" so she wrote a note: "Thank you, dear God, for helping us to locate the trouble." Within twenty-four hours the trouble had been remedied.

A relative had looked for months for a job to no avail. The wife suddenly remembered to write a thank you note and put it in the box: "Thank you God for a good position with steady income for this relative." Within two weeks the relative had the best job of her life, after having looked for work for months.

The children in this family often wrote out notes about the more mundane things of life: Their desire for school clothes, ice cream for dinner, or going swimming. Each week, when they reviewed their notes, they were amazed to find how many of these things had been supplied.

About this "thank you box" method the mother said later, "In our family we have learned to use this 'thank you box' in solving all problems. It has become a necessity in our household. By giving thanks *before* we receive, our problems have often been solved."

HOW SIXTEEN REQUESTS WERE FULFILLED THROUGH THE "THANK YOU BOX" METHOD

A friend from Michigan wrote:

"I began to use the 'thank you box' method six months ago, and it is amazing how many of the desires I wrote out and placed in that box have come true!

"I use cards placing the date of the desire being asked for on the lefthand side. I write out my request in the center, and I place on the right hand side of the card the date by which I want that desire accomplished.

"In these six months, sixteen of my requests have come to pass! They include physical healing, adjustments in business and family matters, financial results, and healings for other people who asked me to pray for them.

"The 'thank you box' method is quite wonderful and I expect to use it as a way of getting results for the rest of my life. It is a simple way to give thanks."

HOW THE "THANK YOU BOX" METHOD WORKED FOR THE AUTHOR

While on a lecture tour of Southern California in the early 1960's, I visited the world famous desert resort of

Palm Springs for the first time. My hostess took me on a whirlwind tour of the area and I fell in love with it.

I exclaimed to her that it was one of the most beautiful areas I had ever visited in my travels, and that I would like to live there some day. She enthusiastically encouraged me to do so. At that time I was widowed, living in modest circumstances in Texas, and there seemed no logical way for me to ever live in Palm Springs.

While in the desert, my hostess introduced me to a friend who insisted upon showing me around her art studio. There I spied an interesting box engraved with palm trees. The artist graciously made me a gift of it, calling it a "prayer box."

From that day forward, I began using it as my "thank you box" dwelling often upon the engraved palm trees on its cover. I moved it with me from place to place as my world gradually improved and expanded over the years. Many of the requests I placed in it came to pass: A larger place of service, a better income, greater vitality, and marriage.

Then almost ten years later, one of the written requests that I had placed in my "thank you box" came to pass, when the way opened for me to move to the desert area to live and to work. One of the first things I did upon my arrival in the desert, was to search out the artist who had first given me that box. She rejoiced with me in the way it had brought my desires to pass. At my request, she again held that little box in her hands and blessed it, declaring that it would always be filled to overflowing with answered prayers.

I shall always treasure that "thank you box" with the

engraved palm trees. It now occupies a place of importance in my study, and it is located only a few feet away from several palm trees that grow just outside my window.

HOW A MARRIAGE IS RESTORED AND A
GOOD JOB OBTAINED

From Canada came this report on the miraculous power of thanksgiving:

"Wonderful things are happening in our lives since I started praising and giving thanks! Everything is falling right into place, and better than we could have ever hoped for.

"Even our originally very confused and hopeless looking marriage situation has now reached a stage that allows both my husband and me to feel at peace and, most of all, helps our children grow up undisturbed by their parents' problems.

"And I have found my right job. I prayed about this for two years. I am now in process of beginning a very special teaching career that will allow me to use my talents the very best way, and to help many people. This is certainly the work I am destined to do. I cannot overestimate the power of praise to straighten out conditions, and to make things right in one's life."

THANKSGIVING SHOULD TAKE DEFINITE
FINANCIAL FORM

Giving thanks in Bible times was not done through mere lip service. It always took definite financial form. During their three annual festivals, the Hebrews' "festival tithes" and other offerings were given as a required part of worship. Not only did the Hebrews observe the act of thanksgiving through their three annual festivals, but in other interesting ways, too:

Before embarking on a journey, going into battle, or facing any challenging situation, the Hebrews gave "faith offerings" to their priests and temples in the faith that their mission would be successful.

After returning from any challenging experience, they went directly to the priest or temple, and gave a "thank offering" in appreciation for the blessings received, and in order to "seal" their new good and make it permanent.

If you have been able to demonstrate greater good in your life, but couldn't hang on to it; or if you have had a hard time getting your prayers answered in the first place, this may be the reason. When was the last time you gave a "faith offering" in anticipation of answered prayer? When was the last time you gave a "thank offering" in appreciation for the blessings already received in order to "seal" that good and make it permanent? *Your acts of thanks should not be done through mere lip service. Your acts of thanks should take definite financial form. too.*

Please note that these special offerings of the Hebrews were given over and above their regular tithes which were given consistently and automatically. The people of Israel gave numerous other offerings too, including a daily offering both morning and evening; a sabbath or weekly offering; a monthly offering; special offerings for Passover; first fruits offerings; meat, drink and sin offerings, etc. *The purpose of these offerings was to keep them in touch with God as the source of their unlimited abundance, and to remind them that there was nothing automatic about the vast blessings they enjoyed.*

Did such lavish giving deplete them? On the contrary! History reveals that the more they gave the more they prospered. And they gave graciously and with joy. They never complained about their vast giving. They could not outgive a rich and loving Father, and they knew it.

A retired couple from Pennsylvania related how the act of thanksgiving in definite financial form helped them. The wife wrote:

"In January of this year, my husband retired because of poor health. Over the years, when they took a collection for any of the other men who retired at work, my husband always gave. Yet when he retired, no collection was taken.

"Several weeks ago, I realized we were not making it financially, and that we must give financially of what we had in order to make room to receive far more.

"So I sent a 'faith offering' and a 'thank offering.' Soon afterwards, my husband's former co-workers took a nice retirement collection for him, and brought it to us! This generous gift helped us get caught up financially. It also assured us of the prospering power there is in giving thanks, both in literal and financial form.

"Giving in faith and with thanksgiving also adds other blessings to one's life. We had been most concerned about our son, who had four impacted wisdom teeth. Upon removing them, the dentist said it was the hardest case he had worked on in a long time. Although he felt terrible for a couple of weeks, our son has now fully recovered. Enclosed is another 'faith offering' and 'thank offering' as expressions of thanksgiving for our present blessings, and for the new good we know is on the way!"

HOW YOU CAN RECEIVE VAST BENEFITS

When problems come to you, it is not because God wants you to have them but because you have been disobedient to the practice of praise and thanksgiving. Through the miraculous act of giving thanks *first,* all obstacles can be overcome.

You can receive the vast benefits available to you from the Prosperity Law of Thanksgiving when you dare to give thanks *first!*

This is the miracle law of prosperity that miraculously clothed and fed the Hebrews during their forty year sojourn in that barren desert. This same miracle law of prosperity can provide for you in your barren periods, too, in ways that seem just as miraculous!

A MEDITATION THAT CAN PRODUCE
PROSPERITY MIRACLES FOR YOU!

"THE DELIBERATE ACT OF THANKS LIBERATES CERTAIN POTENT ENERGIES OF MIND AND BODY THAT ARE NOT OTHERWISE RELEASED. THE DELIBERATE ACT OF THANKSGIVING CAN COMPLETELY TRANSFORM MY LIFE.

"PEOPLE SOMETIMES NEGLECT TO GIVE THANKS FOR SO LONG THAT THINGS GET VERY BAD FOR THEM. MOST OF US HAVE HAD HARDSHIPS BECAUSE WE NEGLECTED TO BE THANKFUL. I CAN INVOKE THE MIRACLE POWER OF THANKSGIVING BY GIVING THANKS *first*, IN THE FACE OF PROBLEMS— BEFORE THERE SEEMS TO BE ANYTHING TO BE THANKFUL FOR.

"SINCE THERE IS PROSPERING POWER IN THANKSGIVING, PEOPLE WHO GIVE THANKS DO NOT STARVE. THEY PROSPER. SO I SPEAK TO THE GOLD IN MY AFFAIRS. I GIVE THANKS THAT DIVINE SUBSTANCE IS AT WORK FOR ME NOW. I GIVE THANKS THAT DIVINE SUBSTANCE DOES EVERYTHING GOOD FOR ME NOW. I GIVE THANKS THAT DIVINE SUBSTANCE SUPPLIES ME, PAYS MY DEBTS, AND IN EVERY WAY BLESSES ME. WITH A LOUD VOICE, I PRAISE DIVINE SUBSTANCE AND CALL IT FORTH AS NEW LIFE, NEW KINDNESS, NEW BOUNTY, AND NEW CONDITIONS. I GIVE THANKS THAT THE PERFECT RESULTS OF DIVINE SUBSTANCE QUICKLY APPEAR IN MY FINANCIAL AFFAIRS NOW.

"I DO NOT LET INGRATITUDE SCARE PROSPERITY AWAY FROM ME. BY GIVING THANKS *first*—BEFORE I RECEIVE—ALL PROBLEMS CAN BE SOLVED. MY ACTS OF THANKSGIVING ARE NOT DONE THROUGH MERE LIP SERVICE. MY ACTS OF THANKS ALSO TAKE DEFINITE FINANCIAL FORM AS 'FAITH OFFERINGS' AND 'THANK OFFERINGS'. YES, THANKSGIVING IS MY MIRACLE POWER FOR PROSPERITY, AND I USE IT OFTEN. I GIVE THANKS AND PROSPER!"

SUMMARY

1. The miracle law of prosperity is released through thanksgiving. The deliberate act of thanks liberates certain potent energies of mind and body that are not otherwise released.

2. Through praise and thanksgiving, you can activate the dynamic powers of the subconscious and superconscious phases of your mind, which then act speedily in your behalf.

3. It is possible through the deliberate act of thanksgiving to completely transform your life. The trick is to give thanks *first,* before there seems to be anything to give thanks for. When you do this, your mental acceptance is accelerated and your good comes more quickly.

4. The Hebrews learned the miracle power of thanksgiving while still in the wilderness. Moses taught them to observe festival days three times a year:

   a) The Passover commemorated their escape out of Egyptian bondage.

   b) "The Feast of the First Fruits" consisted of a day set aside at the *beginning* of each harvest season.

   c) "The Feast of the Tabernacle" was an ingathering at the *close* of the harvest season.

5. The miracle power of thanksgiving is released by praising and giving thanks *before* there seems to be anything to praise and give thanks for! (Symbolized by their *second* annual festival.) It can be the turning point from a mediocre way of life to one of lasting success for you if you dare to do this.

6. If substance does not increase for you, it may be because you have been ungrateful and cynical. Ingratitude can scare prosperity away from you.

7. There is prospering power in thanksgiving. People who give thanks do not starve. They prosper. This is shown in the fact that the two most affluent countries in the world today are the United States and Canada. They are also the *only* two countries in the world that observe a national day of Thanksgiving annually!

8. People sometimes neglect to give thanks for so long that things get very bad for them. Most of us have had hardships because we neglected to be thankful.

9. You can invoke the miracle power of thanksgiving by giving thanks in the face of your problems, *before* there seems to be anything to be thankful for. However, your acts of thanks should not be done through mere lip service. Your acts of thanks should take definite financial form, too, through "faith offerings" and "thank offerings."

10. One family used the "thank you box" method with amazing results on all levels of their life. You can, too. When problems come to you, it is not because God wants you to have them but because you have been disobedient to the practice of praise and thanksgiving. Through the act of giving thanks *first,* all obstacles can be overcome.

THE PROSPERITY LAW
OF PREPARATION

— Chapter 9 —

At the turn of the century, the cattle business was still considered the best way to make a fortune in the great Southwestern part of the United States. In 1901 a group of oil prospectors had a hard time convincing a Texas rancher to lease them some land on which to drill for oil. This rancher was unimpressed with the financial potential of oil. He was satisfied to continue making a living through cattle ranching.

True to their word, the prospectors struck oil on his land. On a hill called "Spindletop" on that historic day—January 10, 1901—the Texas oil industry was born. Instead of rejoicing, the cattle rancher complained to neighbors, "Those fellows have ruined my ranchland, spraying it with that dirty black oil." Later known as "black gold," that dirty black oil made him an instant millionaire, but this rancher did not appreciate his good fortune at first. He had not been mentally prepared to receive it.

HOW MOSES USED THE LAW OF PREPARATION

Moses knew about the prosperity law of preparation. He knew that while the Hebrews were still in the wilderness amid barren experiences, they must begin to mentally prepare to receive their future blessings. Otherwise, they would not be able to recognize and accept those blessings when they came.

In the eighth chapter of the Book of Deuteronomy, Moses used the prosperity law of preparation. The Book of Deuteronomy is one of the most majestic, fascinating and practical books of the Bible. The word "Deuteronomy" means "repetition of the law." Toward the end of his life, Moses reminded the Hebrews of how far they had come. He then described in detail the abundance that awaited them in their Promised Land.

First he described their hard experiences:

"Jehovah thy God hath led thee these forty years in the wilderness . . . and humbled thee, and suffered thee to hunger, and fed thee with manna which thou knewest not . . . that He might make thee to know man doth not live by bread alone, but by every word that proceedeth out of the mouth of Jehovah doth man live."

(Deuteronomy 8:2, 3)

Moses pointed out that hard times are actually periods of inner preparation for the greater good to come: "As a man chasteneth his son, so Jehovah thy God chasteneth thee." (Deuteronomy 8:5) The word "chasten" means "to make better," "to perfect," "to correct."

Moses described how his followers had been divinely provided for even in their wilderness experiences: "Thy raiment waxed not old upon thee, neither did thy foot swell these forty years." (Deuteronomy 8:4)

Moses then invoked the prosperity law of preparation by describing the vast abundance that awaited the Hebrews, once they were prepared to receive it and claim it. Moses described in detail the fertile, prosperous Land of Canaan, even while his followers were still living in the wilderness and provided with manna, just one day at a time. Moses knew they must mentally prepare for their Promised Land while still in that barren place.

He described it to them in vivid detail:

"Jehovah thy God bringeth thee into a good land, a land full of brooks of water, of fountains and springs, flowing forth in valleys and hills."

(Deuteronomy 8:7)

Waters flowing forth from brooks and springs, out of the valleys and hills seemed a wonderful thing to the Hebrews who were living in a dry, waterless desert.

Moses went even further in invoking the prosperity law of preparation: *Not only was there to be an abundance of water, but there was to be an abundance of everything:*

"A land of wheat, barley, vines, fig trees, pomegranates; a land of olive trees and honey; a land wherein thou shalt eat bread without scarceness, thou shalt not lack anything in it; a land whose stones are iron, and out of whose hills thou mayest dig copper. Thou

shalt eat and be full, and thou shalt bless Jehovah thy
God for the good land which He hath given thee."
(Deuteronomy 8:8-10)

It was a great step forward for the Hebrews to expect to
go into a land where there would be no lack. This was
something they had never experienced. There had been
lavish abundance in Egypt but not for them. Even though
the Hebrews had been considered "well-to-do" in the wilderness, there had been barrenness all around them.

HOW YOU CAN USE THE PROSPERITY LAW OF
   PREPARATION

*It is when you are still living in the barren areas of life
that you must prepare for the good you want. If you do not
prepare for your expanded good, then, you will never receive it because you will not be able to recognize it or accept it when it comes.*

The word "prepare" means "to make ready." Here is
the prosperity law of preparation:

*Get ready for the good you want. Become receptive to
its possibilities even before there is any evidence of it. In
your barren wilderness experience, dare to foresee and prepare for it. This opens the way mentally for it to appear.*

A good friend, Dr. Ernest Wilson, has often told the story
of a farmer who became very rich when oil was discovered
on his land. He asked his wife, "Now that we are rich,
what would you like me to buy you?"

"A new milk pail," was her reply. She had not prepared for abundance and did not recognize it when it came.

If you desire more good in your life and it has not come, you may be like that farmer's wife. You may not be prepared for it and you may not recognize it when it appears.

HOW HE PREPARED FOR A NEW CAREER MENTALLY FIRST

A young businessman wanted to enter the ministry, but with a growing family to support, it seemed financially impossible. As the desire persisted, he quietly prepared anyway by attending night school and by taking correspondence courses to complete certain requirements. He even made a sermon preparation file. Every time he read a book, magazine article or newspaper item that interested him, he clipped it for his sermon file.

After quietly preparing for his desired profession in these ways over a period of time, a person of wealth made him a financial gift that covered his seminary training. When he became a minister, he drew heavily upon the sermon materials he had secretly gathered and filed years earlier.

HOW A WIFE'S PREPARATION HELPED HER HUSBAND BECOME A MILLIONAIRE

At the time a housewife learned about the prosperity law of preparation, she and her husband were living in a one room apartment, barely surviving on a limited income.

Since she wanted a lovely home, she decided she must prepare for it by making the most of what she had—that one room. She purchased curtain material for ten cents a yard and beautified that one room.

Soon afterwards, her husband got some ideas for electrical inventions, and quietly patented his ideas. They began to prosper. Every time they moved into larger quarters, she deliberately beautified their living area from her allowance. As she persisted in preparing for wealth, her husband became a millionaire from his inventions. They now own homes all over the world.

Once they wanted a home located on an island. Since there was no island in the desired area, they *built* it and then had their dream house constructed on it! This lady said, "Although we now own homes all over the world, it all began after I prepared for it by fixing up that first one room apartment."

HOW A JOBLESS MAN PREPARED TO BECOME A
MILLIONAIRE

A millionaire businessman says his fortunes turned after he used the law of preparation at the height of the Depression in the 1930's. Jobless, he was living in a rented room with his widowed mother. It was only after he made a "Wheel of Fortune" picturing himself as a wealthy executive that he was offered a steady job. He took it at a time when no one was getting work.

He was so good in his new job he was soon offered a partnership in the company. He took it and worked dili-

gently to help make it a thriving nationwide business.
A few years ago he sold his interest in the company and
retired a millionaire. He stated, "My success began after
I mentally prepared for it by first picturing it on that Wheel
of Fortune while I was still living in one room." (Instructions for making a Wheel of Fortune are given in my book,
The Millionaires of Genesis.)

HOW TO DRAW YOUR GOOD OUT OF THE INVISIBLE

*Begin now to make friends mentally with the good you
want. Consciously and deliberately prepare for it. You must
become conscious of the good you want before you can ever
experience it.*

*When you notice the good you want and deliberately
appreciate it, you make mental contact with it. You begin
drawing it to you on the invisible plane. When you have
noticed it enough, so that you have drawn it close enough
to you on the invisible level, it then manifests quickly. The
thing you prepared for comes upon you. The thing you appreciated overtakes you!*

HOW SHE MARRIED A POPULAR BACHELOR

A young career woman decided she wanted to be married
to an eligible bachelor whom she had known for some time.
Friends often said, "It's too bad that John is a 'confirmed
bachelor' and will never marry."

Instead of accepting these opinions, this young woman made a Wheel of Fortune which pictured her married to this, her dream man. She quietly continued to date this bachelor. She said nothing of her pictured desires, which she viewed daily.

One day while picturing this desired marriage on her Wheel of Fortune, she got a strong feeling that it was accomplished on the invisible and that she should quietly prepare for it in outer ways.

She bought a charm bracelet which contained only one charm—a wedding bell. She wore it daily as a reminder that marriage was near, though she mentioned this possibility to no one. Gradually, she bought a complete wedding trousseau and got her business affairs in order so that a sudden change could be made gracefully.

When she had secretly completed all of these details, the bachelor quietly proposed without warning one night over dinner. They were married ten days later. Theirs has been a happy marriage, though friends of the groom continue to say, "I just don't understand what got into John. He is not the marrying kind."

HOW TO MAKE A MOVE TOWARD THE PROSPERITY YOU WANT

The prosperity law of preparation is this: *Make a move toward your desired good by preparing for it. Then your good will make a move toward you.*

A businessman needed a car. He reasoned that he should prepare for it by building a carport to house it. By the time he had finished the carport, the way opened financially to purchase the car.

The word "desire" in its root means "of the Father." *The good you desire desires you! Everything you want wants you! Desire is divine. It is divinely implanted within you by a loving Father as a means of propelling you into growth and progress. The same Power that gave you the desire will show you how to manifest it, if you can mentally accept that desire and go in its direction. When you have completely prepared for the good you want, it will overtake you—either in the form you expect or in a form infinitely better than you had dared to anticipate.*

HOW THE AUTHOR VISITED A CERTAIN AREA AFTER PREPARING TO DO SO

I wanted to visit a certain area. To do so would require a special wardrobe. It occurred to me that I should prepare for that trip by buying the clothes I would need.

After their purchase, they were hung in the closet as though they might be needed at any time. The method worked. Within a few weeks, an invitation was extended for me to visit that area. The experience I had prepared for overtook me and proved to be a pleasant one.

HOW A BUSINESSMAN PREPARED FOR A NEW WARDROBE AND GOT IT

A businessman had wanted a better wardrobe, but with a growing family to care for, there seemed no money for new clothes. He decided to prepare for a better wardrobe in the faith that it would appear. In preparation, he gave away a number of his old business suits. His wife questioned the wisdom of cleaning out his clothes closet so thoroughly, but he assured her, "We have to prepare for what we want by making room for it."

His method worked. A brother quickly gave him three new suits, though this brother had never given him anything before. This was a fine start on his new wardrobe.

You must prepare your consciousness for the inflow of universal substance. Just as does water or any other visible thing, substance obeys the law of nature and flows into the place prepared for it.

HOW DELIBERATE PREPARATION BROUGHT HER A HOME

Preparation is one of the most practical factors in getting results. All prayers for results amount to nothing if preparation has not been made to receive.

A widow lived for several years in one room with her children. Though she worked hard at her job, no way opened for more suitable living quarters. While pondering her dilemma, she realized that she had done nothing to prepare for better living conditions.

She invoked the prosperity law of preparation in these ways:

First. She made a Wheel of Fortune picturing the kind of home she wanted and she viewed it daily.

Second. Realizing she must do something in an outer way to convince herself this home was possible, she bought a deluxe cook book. A friend helped her invoke the law of preparation by giving her a beautiful set of china dishes, a service for eight.

Third. She sought out a noted portrait painter and commissioned him to do portraits of her children. He agreed to leave them hanging in his studio while she continued to prepare for a home.

Fourth. She spoke these words daily: *"I have a divine right to the best. I now trust my divine rights to bring me out right in experiencing the best. I am beautifully and appropriately housed with the rich substance of the universe now."*

Soon an inheritance made possible the purchase of a home, complete with new furnishings. In less than a year from the time she had begun to prepare for it, she had moved her children from one room into their new home. The portraits, china, and the deluxe cookbook found their rightful place in these elegant new surroundings.

DO SOMETHING TO SHOW YOU EXPECT RESULTS

When you want more good in your life, do something to show you expect it!

A widowed mother was embarrassed about an indelicate problem: She had only two teeth left. Since she had no money for a permanent dental plate, her predicament had caused her much anguish.

Finally she realized she must do something to prepare for
dentures, so she boldly had her dentist remove her last
two teeth. When she heard that her son was coming home
from a tour of duty overseas her first reaction was, "I should
not have gotten rid of those two teeth. What will my son
think when he sees me?" Her later reaction was, "I acted
on faith so it must have been right." She dismissed the
matter in anticipation of his visit.

When the young serviceman arrived, he took one look at
his mother and made her a gift of money for the completion
of her dental work.

*Change your expectancies and you change your life, be-
cause the things you expect come to you.* To help expand
your expectancies declare often: *"Vast improvement comes
quickly in every phase of my life. Something glorious will
happen to me today."* Then do something to show that you
expect those kind of results.

MOSES' PROSPERITY WARNING

In pointing out the prosperity law of preparation, Moses
first reminded the Hebrews that their hard experiences had
been times of inner preparation for the good they wanted.

Second. He prepared them psychologically to receive that
good by describing the lavish abundance that awaited
them in their Promised Land.

Third. In the last half of the eighth chapter of Deuteronomy, Moses warned the Hebrews that all the blessings
they prepared for and received could be taken from them,

if they became overconfident and forgot the source of their wealth:

"When thou hast eaten and art full, and hast built goodly houses and dwelt therein; when thy herds and flocks multiply and thy silver and gold is multiplied and all thou hast is multiplied . . . If thou shalt forget Jehovah thy God . . . ye shall surely perish."

(Deuteronomy 8:12, 19)

After preparing for and receiving your desired good, do not risk losing it by becoming overconfident. Continue to recognize God as the source of all your blessings, if you wish to retain them. Continue turning to Him for guidance, so that you will remain in your Promised Land. Remind yourself often: *"I will remember Jehovah God, for it is He that giveth me power to experience wealth."*

Moses reminded the Hebrews that if they began to think, "My power and the might of my hand hath gotten me this wealth" (Deuteronomy 8:17) they would revert to a state of lack again.

HOW A SCHOOLTEACHER MADE, THEN LOST, A FORTUNE

It happened to a schoolteacher. She used the prosperity laws described in this book and they worked. She inherited a fortune. But she refused to go all the way after receiving this vast legacy by putting God first financially. Although she knew the vast benefits of it, she did not tithe from her windfall, reasoning that to do so would be giving "too much." (She had previously tithed from a much smaller income.)

Instead, she placed her sizeable inheritance in a savings account and enjoyed the interest income from it for several years. Then an ambitious businessman convinced her to withdraw all of it and allow him to invest it for her. Within a matter of weeks, those investments went bad and she lost everything.

When she reverted to a state of lack again, a friend reminded her that she had refused to share *any* of her fortune with God, the source of it, and that she had consequently lost all of it. After learning this bitter lesson, she followed the friend's suggestion and began tithing from her only channel of income left—her paycheck from school-teaching. She is again prospering but has a long way to go before enjoying the vast wealth that had once been bestowed upon her.

As Moses pointed out in the 8th chapter of Deuteronomy, people who put God first financially prosper in good times and in lean ones, because they are divinely protected and guided in the wise use of their substance. Whereas, those who do not honor God with their tithes are not surrounded by an aura of divine protection, and it is much more difficult for them to become permanently prospered.

BLESSINGS OR CURSES—ITS UP TO YOU

This prosperity secret is so important that Moses again pointed it out in the 28th chapter of the Book of Deuteronomy.

First. Moses set out in detail the many blessings in health, human relationships, protection and prosperity that would come to the Hebrews and "overtake" them if they turned to God often for guidance and supply:

"Blessed shalt thou be in the city, and blessed shalt thou be in the field.

Blessed shall be the fruit of thy body, and the fruit of thy ground.

And the fruit of thy beasts, the increase of thy cattle, and the young of thy flock.

Blessed shall be thy basket and thy kneading trough.

Blessed shall thou be when thou comest in, and blessed shalt thou be when thou goest out . . .

Jehovah will command the blessing upon thee in thy barns, and in all that thou puttest thy hand unto;

And he will bless thee in the land which Jehovah thy God giveth thee . . .

And Jehovah will make thee plenteous for good in the fruit of thy body, and in the fruit of thy cattle, and in the fruit of thy ground, in the land which Jehovah swore unto thy fathers to give thee.

Jehovah will open unto thee his good treasure the heavens, to give the rain of thy land in its season, and to bless all the work of thy hand."

(Deuteronomy 28:3-6, 8, 11-12)

Second. Moses then described all of the "curses"— the problems, troubles, difficulties—that would come to those who did not turn to God for their guidance and supply:

"But it shall come to pass, if thou wilt not hearken unto the voice of Jehovah thy God,

To do all his commandments and his statutes which
I command thee this day,

That all these curses shall come upon thee, and overtake thee.

Cursed shalt thou be in the city, and cursed shalt
thou be in the field.

Cursed shall be thy basket and thy kneading-trough.

Cursed shall be the fruit of thy body, and the fruit
of thy ground, the increase of thy cattle, and the young
of thy flock.

Cursed shalt thou be when thou comest in, and
cursed shalt thou be when thou goest out . . .

Because thou served not Jehovah thy God with joy-
fulness, and with gladness of heart, by reason of the
abundance of all things.

Therefore thou serve thine enemies that Jehovah
shall send against thee, in hunger, and in thirst, and in
nakedness, and in want of all things."

(Deuteronomy 28:15-19, 47-48)

WHY HE LOST A FORTUNE

A business executive used the prosperity laws described
in this book and he prospered mightily. But he was too
tight-fisted to go all the way and put God first financially
through tithing "by reason of the abundance of all things."

The result was that he worked day and night until the
diagnosis of an incurable illness slowed him down. He had
family problems and personnel problems in his business. He
gave far more than a tenth of his income to doctors, hos-
pitals, lawyers, and in unexpected business expense and

legal entanglements. He experienced most of the "curses" described by Moses—all of which were of his own tight-fisted making. He would not give to the *constructive* experiences of life, so he had to give to the *destructive* experiences of life, because giving is the law of the universe.

HOW TO AVOID CURSES AND CLAIM BLESSINGS

The suffering and affliction described by Moses came upon those who were disobedient to the law of joy and gladness. The gripers never got into the Promised Land. Those who began griping after they arrived in the wilderness experienced the "curses" predicted by Moses—all of which were of their own making.

You can avoid the curses and claim the blessings described by Moses. For this purpose meditate upon and declare often some of the rich promises listed in the majestic Book of Deuteronomy—especially those found in Chapters 8 and 28.

It is through such "repetition of the Law" (which is what the word "Deuteronomy" means) that you can avoid the curses and claim the rich blessings of life!

A MEDITATION TO HELP YOU INVOKE THE PROSPERITY LAW OF PREPARATION

"IT IS WHEN I AM LIVING IN THE BARREN AREAS OF LIFE THAT I MUST PREPARE FOR THE GREATER GOOD I WANT. IF I DO NOT PREPARE FOR MY EXPANDED GOOD, THEN I WILL NOT BE ABLE TO RECOGNIZE IT OR ACCEPT IT WHEN IT COMES. ALL PRAYERS FOR RESULTS AMOUNT TO NOTHING IF PREPARATION IS NOT MADE TO RECEIVE.

"SO I NOW GET READY FOR THE GOOD THAT I WANT! I NOW MAKE FRIENDS MENTALLY WITH THE GOOD THAT I WANT. I BECOME RECEPTIVE TO ITS POSSIBILITIES EVEN BEFORE THERE IS ANY EVIDENCE OF IT. I DARE TO FORESEE AND PREPARE FOR IT EVEN IN THE MIDST OF BARREN EXPERIENCES. THIS OPENS THE WAY MENTALLY FOR THAT INCREASED GOOD TO APPEAR. YES, THE BLESSINGS I PREPARE FOR COME UPON ME. THE GOOD I APPRECIATE NOW OVERTAKES ME!"

SUMMARY

1. In the 8th chapter of the Book of Deuteronomy, Moses used the prosperity law of preparation. The Book of Deuteronomy is one of the most majestic, fascinating and practical books in the Bible. The word "Deuteronomy" means "repetition of the law." Toward the end of his life, Moses reminded the Hebrews how far they had come. He then described the abundance that awaited them in their Promised Land (Deuteronomy 8) if they continued to use the laws of success he had taught them.

2. Moses knew that while the Hebrews were still in the wilderness amid barren experiences, they must begin mentally to prepare to receive their future blessings. Otherwise, they would not be able to recognize and accept those blessings when they came.

3. Moses pointed out that the hard times the Hebrews had been through were actually periods of inner preparation for the great good to come.

4. Moses then prepared the Hebrews for the wealth that was to come by describing in detail the abundance of water, land, wheat, barley, vines, crops that were to be theirs in their Promised Land: "Thou shalt eat bread without scarceness. Thou shalt not lack anything."

5. Moses then described the wealth of the Promised Land: A rich land of iron, copper. "Thou shalt eat and be full, and thou shalt bless Jehovah thy God for the good land which He hath given thee."

6. Likewise it is when you are still living in the barren areas of life that you must prepare for the good you

want. If you do not prepare for your expanded good then, you will never receive it because you will not be able to recognize it or accept it when it comes.

7. Get ready for the good you want. Become receptive to its possibilities even before there is any evidence of it. In your wilderness experiences, dare to foresee and prepare for it. This opens the way mentally for it to appear.

8. Begin now to make friends mentally with the good you want. Consciously and deliberately prepare for it. You must become conscious of the good you want before you can ever experience it. When you notice the good you want and deliberately appreciate it, you make mental contact with it. You begin drawing it to you on the invisible plane. When you have noticed it enough, it then manifests quickly. The thing you prepared for comes upon you. The thing you appreciated overtakes you.

9. The good you desire desires you! Everything you want wants you. When you have completely prepared for the good you want, it will overtake you. Preparation is one of the most practical factors in getting results. All prayer for results amounts to nothing if preparation has not been made to receive it.

10. In the last half of the 8th chapter of Deuteronomy, Moses warned the Hebrews that all the blessings they prepared for and received could be taken from them, if they became over-confident and forgot the source of their wealth. Again in Deuternonomy 28, Moses pointed out in detail the many blessings that would come to the Hebrews and "overtake" them if they turned to God often for guidance and supply. He warned of the "curses" that would come if they did not. In these ways Moses thoroughly prepared his followers for a successful future.

THE PROSPERITY LAW
OF COMPLETION

— Chapter 10 —

If you have worked inwardly and outwardly to realize certain blessings in your life—and they have not appeared—it may be because you are now ready to use the prosperity law of completion.

At the close of Moses' life, we find the "Song of Moses." (Deuteronomy 32) It was a song of completion. This outstanding leader—the greatest of the Old Testament and one of the greatest of all times—had the good sense to know when he had completed a cycle and his work was finished.

In his famous "Song of Moses" he reviewed all his accomplishments and reminded the Hebrews of all he had led them through. He told them his work was done and he spoke the word of completion.

Historians describe the "Song of Moses" as a death song. But the word "death" symbolizes completion, the ending of an era. Moses knew he must speak the word of completion and let go, as he felt a change near. He knew he must look upon every ending as a new beginning.

*How often you may have missed your good because you
did not know how to sing the "Song of Moses." You may
have kept fretting and trying to force your good when you
should have spoken the word of completion, and then let go.*

It would seem that Moses had every right to fret and
to try to force results. To all appearances his objective had
not been reached: His people had not yet entered their
Promised Land. Even though he had tried diligently to take
them, they had not been ready to go.

WHY JOSHUA AND CALEB HAD BEEN RESTRAINED

You will recall that early in his wilderness experiences
Moses had sent twelve spies, including Joshua and Caleb,
into the Promised Land to spy on its inhabitants and to
check on its resources. The two prosperous thinkers in the
group, Joshua and Caleb, had returned elated, "Let us go
up at once and possess it. We are well able to take it" had
been their report. (Numbers 13:30) But the other ten spies
had brought back an entirely different report. They claimed
the people of the Promised Land were giants and uncon-
querable. Because of their negative attitudes, Moses had
decided not to pursue taking the Promised Land at that
point.

Now, sometime later, the best Moses could hope to do
was to lead the Hebrews to the edge of the wilderness in
sight of their Promised Land of Canaan. He realized that
with that accomplished, his work would be done.

Metaphysically, Moses symbolizes knowledge of the laws
of success and prosperity, whereas Joshua symbolizes love of

those laws and their use. Like Moses, we can claim freedom from a great deal of bondage in our lives through gaining a knowledge of the laws of prosperity and success. That knowledge can lead us out of bondage and to the very edge of our Promised Land. But it takes Joshua's love of the laws of prosperity and success, and his fearless use of them, to carry us forward in making our Master Demonstration of getting into and staying in our Promised Land of unlimited good. (You will find a chapter on the prosperity secrets of Joshua and Caleb in my book, *The Millionaire Joshua.*[1])

SPEAK THE WORD OF COMPLETION

The word "completion" means "lacking in nothing, whole, full, entire, finished, concluded, perfected, ended, accomplished." *If there is something in your life you have tried unsuccessfully to make whole, full, entire, perfect— yet have been unable to—dare to speak the word of completion. Then loose it and let it go.*

Sometimes it is only after one works diligently, then relaxes and lets go, that the work comes to fruition. An Oriental proverb describes it: "The flower of Truth blooms in the silence after the storm and stress of effort."

The Sabbath Day of the Creation Story emphasizes the necessity for a time of cessation of effort, a time of relaxing and letting things work out.

When you have done all you know how to do in inner and outer ways to solve any problem, or to create new good,

1. Published 1977 (DeVorss & Company, Marina del Rey, Calif)

and still results have not come—that is the time to release and cease further effort. There are halting places in mental action. These are the times to speak nothing, think nothing, do nothing. You have already spoken the word of prosperity, success, completion. Now let it alone.

Moses knew this. He had hoped to get the Hebrews out of the barren wilderness. He had hoped to get them into the Promised Land. He had failed on both counts. Yet he knew he had done all he could. Moses realized that *when you have done all you can about a situation, then you have done all you are supposed to do. Speak the word of completion and let go. That opens the way for results to appear.*

HOW THE WORD OF COMPLETION BROUGHT CHANGE OF JOBS

Once when I had completed my work in a certain job, I knew that I was ready for a complete change. I felt the restlessness and discontent that wells up within when a change is near.

But I could not get free of that job. Nothing new opened to me when I made other contacts. I used every success law I knew in an attempt to get free of the old situation. Still nothing happened.

One day after praying again for guidance, I found these words: *"The work of my hands and the plans of my life are now moving quickly toward a sure and perfect completion. I anticipate the good. In God's right action, I now place my full trust."*

The word "completion" stood out. That was the idea I had been searching for. Along with these words I also began to decree: *"This is a time of divine completion. Miracles now follow miracles and wonders never cease."* I did nothing more about the problem.

An offer of another job that I had long desired soon came. But nothing had happened until I had spoken the word of completion and turned the matter loose.

AN OCCULT FORMULA FOR RESULTS

There is an occult formula for obtaining results:

Think, act, wait. Don't miss your good by not waiting. People often reach a place in their progress where it seems impossible for them to attain their heart's desires, no matter how hard they try. Usually, close observation reveals that those people have tried so hard mentally, and perhaps physically, that they are under severe mental and emotional strain.

They have become tense and anxious, rarely relaxing. They have generated a strained vibration which has built up an inharmonious wall around them. This invisible shell of tension is being radiated out from them to others. It is repelling the very good they have worked so hard trying to attain.

Just as soon as this invisible wall of tension can be dissolved, the things these people desire will be able to get through to them. Such people need to relax, let go, get into a pleasant frame of mind and then just wait. This breaks up the hard shell and their desires are then able to materialize.

HOW THEY PROSPERED WHEN THINGS GOT TIGHT FINANCIALLY

A businesswoman and her husband went into business on a shoestring. They discovered that when their product was not selling and when their customers were not paying, it was usually because this woman and her husband had gotten tense about business affairs. Their tension had been unconsciously communicated to their customers, who were repelled by their anxiety.

These people discovered that if, when things got tight financially, they would take whatever money was on hand and leave town for a few days to rest and relax, upon their return customers would be clamoring for their product. The mail would be full of checks.

If you failed to attain your heart's desire, though you have worked long and hard to do so, this may be the reason. Dare to relax and let go all cares for awhile. Speak the word of completion and then let the situation alone. Even Jehovah enjoyed a Sabbath after a period of creative effort. You can hardly afford to do less if you wish to expand the good in your life.

Declaring *"It is finished,"* when there is no visible evidence of it has the power to bring the desired good into visibility. Persistent decrees that *"It is done, and it is now made visible,"* can bring into view whatever one asks or desires. To say *"It is done"* when there is no sign of results is the way to obtain results!

HOW A DOCTOR MANIFESTED SUPPLY

After learning the inner laws of prosperity, a metaphysician felt led to stop sending monthly bills to her clients. Instead of making specific charges, she decided to work on "a love offering" basis. She wanted to help all who came for help regardless of their financial status.

For two years she worked faithfully on this financial basis, and though she helped countless numbers of people, she almost starved. Even when she was faint from lack of food, she felt her decision had been the right one.

One day when she felt she could not endure the privation any longer, she prayed for guidance. The answer came: "You have not spoken the word of supply. You have not spoken the word of completion." She began to declare: *"It is done. God is now manifested as my supply."*

A stranger soon walked into her office and gave her several thousand dollars. Her problem of supply was over! She said she never had to meet that problem again.

HOW TO GET THROUGH A TRANSITION PERIOD

Jesus declared completion on the cross before his agony ended. How quickly the suffering left Him after He decreed in a loud voice, *"It is finished."* (John 19:30)

If you are suffering in some way, if you are in a transition period between the old and the new, then decree for the old even though it doesn't appear to be true: *"It is finished. It is done now quickly and in peace."* These words can release miracle power for you that will complete an old cycle quickly. They will also unlock the doors to your new good quickly.

Dare to say: *"God's work is finished in this situation and it manifests now. I see only completion now."* Or paraphrase the words of Jesus: *"The time is fulfilled. My good is at hand and manifests now."* (from Mark 1:14)

HOW A COLLEGE STUDENT PROVED THIS

A college student was long overdue in getting his master's degree. Events seemed to have conspired against its completion. His mother, who was faced with the financial obligation of educating her son, realized that someone needed to speak the word of completion for this frustrating, expensive delay. She began to write and to declare these words every day: *"The time is fulfilled. The finished results manifest in this situation now, quickly and in peace."*

Almost immediately, her son decided upon a subject for his master's thesis and began the research and writing of it. Within a short time he had obtained his master's degree, had gotten a job, and was finally supporting himself.

WHY YOU MUST ALSO LET GO THE PLEASANT CYCLES

It is easy to say to the unpleasant cycles in life, *"It is finished. It is done. It is completed."* But you have to let go the pleasant cycles too, when they have served their purpose, if you are to move on into larger experiences.

People sometimes stop their progress because they will not release a good cycle that is completed. They continue to think about, talk about and hold to those pleasant memories, as though they were to be the last.

Your good is not static. Your good is progressive. Your good evolves and changes. You must allow it to evolve. You must change with it. You must be willing to release accustomed forms of good when your progress or that of another demands it.

Emerson has said that you must be willing to let the angels go out of your life so that archangels can come in— even when you cannot see where the archangels are coming from, or what form they will take.

Moses had been an angel to the Hebrew people. He had gotten them out of Egyptian bondage and through the wilderness. But they had to release him so that their archangel, Joshua, could take command and lead them into their Promised Land.

Loosing your good, freeing it readily, when you have outgrown it, requires courage. But nothing remains the same. Change is the law of the universe. Everything changes. A blade of grass will not be the same tomorrow as it is today. Neither will you. Scientists say you have changed so much that there is not a single cell in your body that was there several months ago.

Indeed, the only thing in life that is certain is change. The inevitability of change is not new. It has been going on at a steady pace for three billion years. When change knocks at your door, you may wish to remind yourself, *"This is a change for the better. I have everything to gain through this change, so I welcome it."*

In the midst of change as you are busy releasing past good, remind yourself that no door ever closes but that a bigger, better one is trying to open. No matter how good the cycle you are completing has been, the new one that is opening can be ever better.

HOW THE ACT OF BLESSING BRINGS COMPLETION

You may think, "But I have done this. I have released the past, both the pleasant and the unpleasant phases. I have been expecting a new door to open but it has not. I have waited and still my new good has not appeared. Why?"

Moses gave the answer. His song of completion is found in the 32nd chapter of Deuteronomy. In the next chapter, you find the blessing that Moses placed upon the Children of Israel. Why did Moses speak the word of completion and later give a final blessing?

He knew that *no experience can ever be finished until you give it your final blessing.* Moses knew he would not be be free of his critical, rebellious followers until he gave them a final blessing.

Have you ever had a negative experience that you could not get freed from? Or one that you were freed from for a time, then it reappeared? Have you ever had the same problem reappear again and again in your life, and you wondered why?

No experience can ever be concluded in your life until you have given it your final blessing. If you do not bless it, that old problem will reappear again and again, awaiting your blessing.

So long as you resent a troublesome person or circumstance, you will have to meet that problem repeatedly in your life in some guise. When you give a blessing to that person or circumstance, then comes your release—often in some dramatic way.

HOW SHE WENT FROM CARETAKER TO A MANAGER'S JOB

A woman had a job as a caretaker for a large boarding house. She detested her work among the pots and pans. When she had tried to get free of this job, it had only gained a stronger hold on her.

In desperation she talked with a friend who said, "What do you want to do?" She replied, "I want to be the head of a large hotel where I can meet people from all parts of the world. I want to entertain them instead of cook and clean for them."

The friend pointed out that this woman was fighting her present place in life and her resentment was holding her there; that nothing is ever gained by fighting. What we fight usually fights back. Use of the following statements was suggested: *"I place myself and all my affairs lovingly in the hands of the Father. That which is for my highest good now comes to me."*

It was a prayer of release and blessing. As this bitter woman declared the words *"Lovingly in the hands of the Father"* for each challenge that confronted her, the way to the job she wanted opened in a most unforeseen way:

Two real estate men appeared at her boarding house on other business. They mentioned that they were looking for someone to manage a large hotel, the nicest in town. This lady got the job and it proved to be a happy change.

But she did not get it until she stopped fretting about her present job. When she released herself and all that concerned her to a loving Father, and when she started blessing all that was unpleasant in her life, the tide turned. Completion of the old came quickly and her new good appeared.

FIND A POINT OF AGREEMENT

Like Moses, you will find that when you dare to give an old situation your blessing, it fades out of your life. Another woman had faced the same problem in different guises many times. Each time she spoke the word of completion. But unlike Moses, she did not give that problem her final blessing.

Finally she realized that she must find a point of agreement with that problem in order to bless it out of her life. She realized that *if you put your condemnation upon anything in life, it will hit back at you and hurt you.* But if you bless it, it has no further power and will fade away. She began to bless and praise the events and the people that had cursed her. She blessed and praised all the periods of hardship and failure through which she had passed. She decreed that these had been periods of pruning and growth.

As Moses must have done when giving a final blessing to his critical followers, she gave thanks for the problem that had appeared so often in her life. This time she gained a sense of peace and release from it. Not only did it fade away, but it has never recurred.

DRAMATIC CHANGES COME ANYWAY

What about those people who hang onto old experiences and do not want to face the challenge of change? What happens to them?

Change comes to them, too, often in the form of shocks. Change cannot be by-passed. It can only be temporarily avoided. The soul demands change for its expansion. *In the midst of change, new good is being created.* If the caterpillar could refuse to change, he would miss becoming a butterfly. The person who tries to avoid change often stagnates and change still comes to him, but in unhappy ways, through experiences of loss, lack, or failure.

When the soul is ready for the next step in its upward growth, great changes often take place. Progressive souls may go through a number of major changes in a lifetime.

You should not let yourself become bound to old ideas, relationships or environments. You should not allow yourself to become so fixed in certain ways of living that you cannot be happy when those ways change as they surely will. As you expand your thinking, old relationships and ways of living drop away from you, only to be replaced by new ones that are more exactly right for you.

In his Essay on *Compensation*,[2] Emerson writes that you should be putting off "dead circumstances" daily. He says that when you resist doing so, your growth comes in shocks. He warns:

> "We do not believe there is any force in today to rival or recreate that beautiful yesterday. We linger in the ruins . . . We sit and weep in vain. The voice of the Almighty saith, 'Up and onward forevermore.' We cannot stay amid the ruins."

The changes you refuse to cooperate with are often forced upon you in a negative way: Through ill health, disappointment, loss of wealth, family or friends. The loss may seem unbearable, but it is for good because it works revolutionary changes in your life. Such changes force the termination of an era that was waiting to be closed. This allows the formation of new ones, more friendly to the growth of the individual.

YOUR SUCCESS FORMULA FOR COMPLETION

If there is something in your life you wish to conclude, remember the formula:

Speak the word of completion. Loose the good as well as the unpleasant. Realize that your good changes and you must change with it. Give that old experience your final blessing in parting, so that it will not come back later to try to get your attention for a final blessing. Ask God's for-

---

2. From *The Writings of Ralph Waldo Emerson*, (New York, N.Y.: Random House, Inc., 1940).

giveness for having resented or found fault with anything or anybody. As you do these things, completion will come. When it does, remember the words of Emerson:[3]

> "Finish each day and be done with it . . . You have done what you could; some blunders and absurdities no doubt crept in; forget them as soon as you can. Tomorrow is a new day. You shall begin it well and serenely."

Use of these success statements will help you to invoke the Prosperity Law of Completion and reap its vast benefits:

"I PLACE MYSELF AND ALL MY AFFAIRS LOVINGLY IN THE HANDS OF THE FATHER. THAT WHICH IS FOR MY HIGHEST GOOD NOW COMES TO ME."

"THIS IS A TIME OF DIVINE COMPLETION. MIRACLES NOW FOLLOW MIRACLES, AND WONDERS NEVER CEASE."

"I NOW ASK GOD'S FORGIVENESS FOR HAVING RESENTED ANYONE OR ANYTHING OF THE PAST OR PRESENT. I GIVE THAT PERSON, SITUATION OR THING MY FINAL BLESSING. THIS BRINGS COMPLETION BETWEEN US NOW AND FOREVER."

"MY GOOD CHANGES AND I WILLINGLY CHANGE WITH IT. I RELEASE THAT WHICH IS PLEASANT AS WELL AS THAT WHICH IS UNPLEASANT FROM MY PAST AND PRESENT.

"I HAVE INVOKED THE PROSPERITY LAW OF COMPLETION AND SATISFYING RESULTS NOW APPEAR."

"I LOOK UPON EVERY ENDING AS A NEW BEGINNING. I AM READY FOR MY NEW GOOD NOW!"

---

3. Ibid.

SUMMARY

1. If you have worked inwardly and outwardly to realize certain blessings in your life—and they have not appeared—it may be because you are now ready to use the prosperity law of completion.

2. At the close of Moses' life is found the "Song of Moses." It is a song of completion. This outstanding leader had the good sense to know when his work was finished.

3. How often you may have missed your good because you did not know how to sing the "Song of Moses." You may have fretted and tried to force your good when you should have spoken the word of completion and then let go.

4. If there is something in your life you have tried unsuccessfully to make right, yet have been unable to, dare to speak the word of completion. Then loose it and let it go.

5. Sometimes it is only after one works diligently, then relaxes and lets go, that the work comes to fruition.

6. When you have done all you can about a situation, then you have done all you are supposed to do. Speak the word of completion and let go. That opens the way for results to appear.

7. There is an occult formula for obtaining results: Think, act, wait. Don't miss your good by not waiting.

8. It is easy to speak words of completion for the unpleasant cycles in life. But you have to let go the pleasant cycles too when they have served their purpose, if you are to move on into larger experiences.

9. Moses' song of completion is found in Deuteronomy 32. In the next chapter is found the blessing that Moses placed upon the Children of Israel. Why did Moses speak the word of completion and then follow with a final blessing? Because no experience can ever be finished until you give it your final blessing. Moses knew he would not be free of his critical, rebellious followers until he gave them a final blessing.

10. Moses had been an angel to the Hebrew people. He had gotten them out of Egyptian bondage and through the wilderness. But they finally had to release him so their archangel, Joshua, could take command and lead them into their Promised Land. Your good evolves and changes. You must change with it. You must be willing to release accustomed forms of good when your progress or that of another demands it. To do so always leads to increased success.

IN CONCLUSION . . . .

YOUR PROSPERITY CHARGE

How To Enter Your Promised Land of Abundance

The great prosperity lesson we learn from Moses is that there must be an "inworking" before there can be an "outworking."

A "charge" usually contains instructions. It points out a duty or responsibility. Jehovah's charge to Joshua, as Joshua prepared to take the reins and lead the Hebrews into their long-desired Promised Land, contains a prosperity charge for you as you conclude this book. It describes the "inworking" that must take place within your own thoughts and feelings, which then leads to the "outworking" or outpicturing of your Promised Land of increased abundance on all levels of your life:

"Only be strong and very courageous, to observe to do according to all the law, which Moses my servant commanded thee; turn not from it to the right hand or to the left, that thou mayest have good success whithersoever thou goest.

"This book of the law shall not depart out of thy mouth, but thou shalt meditate thereon day and night, that thou mayest observe to do according to all that is written there; *for then thou shalt make thy way prosperous, and then thou shalt have good success.*"

(Joshua 1:7, 8)

I trust that as you persistently use the prosperity laws described in this book: *"Then shalt thy way be made prosperous, and thou shalt have good success!"*

SPECIAL NOTE:

You will enjoy studying the companion book to this one entitled *"The Millionaire Joshua, His Prosperity Secrets for You."*